HOME ECONOMICS

How to eat like a king on a budget

JANE ASHLEY

Photography by Phil Ashley

Disclaimer: The information in this book should not be treated as a substitute for professional medical advice. If you require gluten-free please carefully check the labels of the products you are buying. Neither the author nor the publisher can be held responsible for any claim or damage arising out of th[e] gestions made in this book. This is a book about

Most of these recipes we'[ ] e will originally have come from my wide colle[ ] been adapted by me to fit our lifestyle and bud[ ]

Raw or semi-cooked eggs [ ], pregnant or breast-feeding women, the elderl[y] [ ]

The shopping list budgets [ ] 017.

10 9 8 7 6 5 4 3 2 1

Copyright © Jane Ashley 2017
Designed by Jane Ashley
Photography © Phil Ashley
Printed in Italy by L.E.G.O. SpA

Published in 2017 by Short Books, Unit 316, ScreenWorks,
22 Highbury Grove, London, N5 2ER

A CIP catalogue record for this book is available from the British Library.

ISBN: 978-1-78072-344-0

Printed in Italy by L.E.G.O. SpA

Contents

WHY DID WE EAT FOR £1 A DAY?

My aim in this book is to show you a way of shopping and cooking that can save you money and still allow you to put delicious food on the table.

I'm not going to patronise or preach; cooking well on a budget and with minimal waster is nothing new, but it's a skill a lot of people, me included, were unaware of or just not taught.

Our grandparents, and their parents too, were able to eat and cook frugally, but at some point in the 70s and 80s – with the age of convenience foods and both parents going out to work – the skill got lost and was never passed on.

About 15 years ago I hardly ever cooked meals from scratch. I never really learnt how to. At school in the 80s all we learnt was how to make pastry and fairy cakes and that was about it. I have never made choux pastry since, although I must say my short-crust is superb!

My mother didn't cook much either: she worked full-time six days a week, and on her one day off she liked to play golf with my dad. I don't blame her – she didn't need to cook. Most companies back then had canteens and school dinners weren't just nuggets and chips; they were proper meals – meat and two veg. In the evening we would have just a sandwich for tea or fish and chips on a Friday.

So without any lessons on how to cook, I struck lucky and married a man whose mother is a very good cook. For the first few years of married bliss I let him do most of the cooking. I'd watch, pour the wine and keep him company. Maybe even chop a vegetable or stir a sauce. When it was my turn to cook, it would be from the freezer, deposited onto a tray and put in the oven at 190°C. Not exciting, and rather costly.

That all changed when we had our daughter. One, we needed to save a bit of money – babies can be quite expensive, and two, I wanted my precious baby to eat only natural, healthy food. New parents, eh?

This also coincided with Jamie Oliver's TV show highlighting the decline of the school dinner. Remember the turkey twizzler? At the time I was working in London and Jamie was doing a book signing nearby for his book *Dinners*. I didn't want to miss out, so duly bought a copy and got it signed. For once the recipes inside didn't look like hieroglyphics. The book explained the mysteries of sautéing and blending. I remember the day we trotted off to the shops, toddler in tow, to buy these exotic ingredients we hadn't used before: Chinese 5 spice, ginger, coriander. Wow! It was a revelation tasting Jamie's noodle stir-fry for the first time. It became a firm favourite and I still cook many of the dishes from that book.

So fast-forward to last year when I was talking to a friend who volunteers at a food bank. Some of her stories of parents trying to feed their families or heat their homes on tiny budgets were heartbreaking. At the same time I became interested in the work of a charity called 'Below the Breadline' which raises awareness about people all over the world living on the equivalent of £1 a day. That got me thinking about my family and how we would manage on such a tight budget.

So I challenged us to eat as a family on £3 a day. On our first challenge we ran out of milk and butter and craved sweet things and there were many hiccups in the days that followed. Since then I've learnt all sorts of new things and managed to add in some treats. There are some standards I won't let slip; for instance I only use free-range eggs. They cost a little more but can still be fitted within the tight budget.

I decided to start a blog (eatnotspend. wordpress.com) about how we got on, mainly to show other people struggling to make ends meet how they could shop on a tiny budget but still eat well. I put all the recipes on the blog so anyone following could recreate the same meals. I also included the shopping lists so they would know exactly what to buy.

I persuaded my husband, a photographer, to help; I think the shots prove that with good lighting and a bit of styling you can make even simple meals look as lovely as they taste.

It was a steep learning curve – not least because I had barely any social media experience at all. But as a graphic designer I found I got huge pleasure out of trying to present the information in as accessible and helpful a way as possible.

After the first week someone requested that I try a vegetarian budget week and, intrigued, I convinced my family to give it a go. This time they were a bit more willing as we had eaten some really nice meals on the challenge. Not knowing much about vegetarian food, I set about working out another menu plan. Since then we've done over a dozen different budget food challenges, including a vegan week and a gluten-free one.

In this book, I allow slightly more than £1 a day each – my target is £35 a week to feed a family of four. I provide day-by-day meal plans which are simple to use and all the recipes are easy to follow. I'm not a professional chef or a nutritionist, but I have cooked enough meals in my life to know a few tips and tricks. I'm a mum who understands that a balanced diet containing enough protein, healthy fats and plenty of fresh fruit and vegetables is a recipe for healthiness and wellbeing. Put it this way: if I can do this, most people can.

TOP TIPS TO SAVE YOU MONEY

1. Always, ALWAYS have a list.

2. Check what you have run out of or need before you write your list. We plan what we are eating on what days and who's working late or who is going to be out, so that we only buy what we will need for that week.

3. Never go shopping when you are hungry; you'll end up buying sweets and snacks.

4. Check your prices, as supermarkets are always putting prices up and down. If it's expensive that week, don't get it. Swap in something else; be flexible.

5. Buy supermarket own brands. I've taste-tested loads and if you use them well, you can't tell the difference. Why pay £2 for something that can cost 35p?

6. If you don't trust yourself not to overspend in the supermarket, order online. That way you can't be tempted and you can see how much you are spending as you go along.

7. When shopping online, some of the budget versions won't appear unless you put in the budget brand name first, for example Morrisons is M Savers, Tesco is Everyday Value, ASDA is Smart Price, Sainsbury's is Basics, Co-op is Simple Value and Waitrose is Essentials. Have a look first to see if it's available.

8. The only date you need to worry about on food packaging is the use-by date, the 'sell-by' is for the supermarkets' own turnaround and the 'best before' is when it's at its optimum freshness, but the 'use by' is when it will go off. Sniff first if you're not sure, but don't mess around with meat or fish or you could get ill.

9. Some people swear by the discounted yellow-sticker items, but I tend not to bother with them. I don't normally buy the sort of products in that section: it's mostly ready-made meals and pork pies, and I don't like the sharp elbows either.

10. Your freezer is your friend. Don't waste food by letting it go off. Most of our meat will go straight in the freezer unless we're eating it the next day. Milk, bread and butter freeze well; cheese can end up a bit crumbly but it's OK for sauces.

11. Try to buy in season when it'll be cheaper; if parsnips are really cheap, get more and make soup and freeze it. I also sometimes make up packs of cooked chopped onions, carrots and celery, then freeze them ready for quick mid-week sauces, risottos and pastas.

12. Grow your own. Even if it's just a few herbs on a windowsill. We only have a small garden, so it's not exactly *The Good Life* but I do get great satisfaction knowing we've eaten our own home-grown food.

STORE CUPBOARD ESSENTIALS

The following is a list of the essential everyday stock cupboard ingredients you will need to make all the weekly menus in this cookbook. They are all standard items, so there should be nothing scary, expensive or difficult to find.

Don't forget: whenever possible, buy the cheaper supermarket own brand.

Salt
Peppercorns
Olive oil
Vegetable oil
Soy sauce
Tabasco
Worcestershire sauce
Tomato sauce
Tomato purée
Brown sauce

Mayonnaise
Sweet chilli sauce
English powdered mustard
Dijon mustard
Honey
Lemon juice
Lime juice
Stock cubes
Plain and self-raising flour
Strong white flour

Dried yeast	Ground ginger	White wine vinegar	**Fresh from the garden:**
Bicarbonate of soda	Nutmeg	Balsamic vinegar	Bay leaves
Raisins	Cloves	Rice wine vinegar	Rosemary
Vanilla Essence	Sweet paprika	Black/yellow mustard	Mint
Cumin seeds	Saffron	seeds	Thyme
Coriander seeds	Turmeric	Dried thyme	Sage
Fennel seeds	Chilli powder	Dried oregano	Oregano
Chinese 5 spice	Garam masala	Dried mint	Parsley
Ground cumin	Mild curry powder	Sunflower/pumpkin seeds	(If you don't have any
Ground coriander	Chilli seeds/flakes	Olives	fresh, just use dried.)
Ground cinnamon	Cayenne pepper	Capers	
Cinnamon sticks	Malt vinegar	Gherkins	

EQUIPMENT ESSENTIALS

If you want to save some serious money, you have to cook from scratch as much as possible and if you have the right equipment this will be a whole lot easier.

The following list comprises the basic tools you'll need for everyday cooking. You've probably got most of them anyway, but if you don't there are some great supermarket own-brand versions out there. You don't need to buy the most expensive. I would

buy good quality knives, though, as cheap wobbly ones can be dangerous.

Remember to buy different colour chopping boards for different ingredients: green for vegetables and fruit, red for raw meat, blue for fish (optional) and white for cooked food. Always clean them in hot soapy water.

2-3 saucepans	Muffin tray	Selection of knives:	Can opener
Stock pot	900g loaf tin	paring, chopping, utility,	3-4 chopping boards
Large frying pan	16cm and 20cm cake tins	chef's, bread knife	Rolling pin
Small frying pan	25cm flan tin	2-3 wooden spoons	Mortar and pestle
Wok	Hand blender/ food	Spatula	Cookie cutter
Colander	processor	Slotted spoon	Oven glove
Sieve	Electric whisk	Masher	Griddle (optional)
Measuring jug	2-3 mixing bowls	Peeler	
Measuring cups/spoons	Scales	Grater	
Roasting tin	Tongs	Garlic crusher	
Baking sheet	Ladle	Lemon press	

HOW TO MAKE FRESH PASTA
the easy way

There's nothing as nice as fresh pasta, but it can be quite expensive to buy in the supermarket. I've never even seen gluten-free or vegan versions, which is such a shame as I feel people on these diets are really missing out. These easy recipes are perfect for everyone.

Serves 4

Ingredients for fresh pasta:
400g plain flour
1 tsp salt
150ml water
2 eggs

Ingredients for fresh vegan pasta:
400g plain flour
1 tsp salt
150ml water

Ingredients for gluten-free pasta:
300g gluten-free bread flour
2 tsp xanthan gum
1 tsp salt
125ml water
1 tbsp oil
2 eggs
(See recipe idea on page 177)

Note:
Traditionally you would use Italian '00' flour, but I normally make mine with just plain flour, and if you're on a budget you don't really want to go buying more expensive flours.

You can make this on a large clean work surface or in a bowl if you prefer.

Combine your dry ingredients and make a well in the centre. Pour in the the water, egg and oil, if using.

Pull in the sides and mix together well, then knead the dough on a floured surface until it goes springy, 5-10 minutes. Add more flour or water if you need to.

Wrap it in clingfilm and place it in the fridge for at least 1 hour.

Now to roll out the dough: if you don't have a pasta machine, a tip I learnt recently was to start at one end and roll a section, then let that hang over the edge of your work surface while you roll out the next bit. Continue in this way until you have rolled it all very thinly, section by section. Make sure not to let it touch the floor.

Once it's rolled out, slice it thinly into strips or alternatively you can use a pasta machine if you have one. I use a special rolling pin with grooves to slice mine – you can get one from a good cook shop or online.

Now put the water on to boil for the pasta. Make sure you use your largest pan so it has room to move.

When the water has boiled, add a pinch of salt and then the pasta, simmer for 3-4 minutes or until it's just soft (6-8 minutes for gluten-free).

Once the pasta is cooked, drain it in a large colander. You can stir in a tablespoonful of olive oil or pesto to stop it sticking together.

SPINACH AND FETA FILLED PASTA

Once you've made your basic pasta dough, you can shape it however you like. Take a look online or in the supermarket for ideas. This recipe is for a mezzaluna-style pasta. I coloured mine in the Italian flag colours using beetroot and blitzed nettle pastes.

Serves 4

Ingredients for the pasta:
400g plain flour
1 tbsp salt
150ml water
2 eggs

Ingredients for the filling:
1 small onion, finely chopped
1 tbsp oil
200g frozen spinach
100g feta, chopped
Salt and pepper

To serve:
Handful of pine nuts
Parmesan shavings

Optional ingredients:
You can naturally colour your pasta green with blanched and blitzed spinach, or pink with roasted and blitzed beetroot. Just add 1 tsp of the purée when you add the water at the dough stage.

First, make up your filling by softening the onion with the oil on a low heat in a saucepan.

Defrost the spinach, squeezing out the liquid, before adding it to the cooked onions. Tip the mixture into a bowl and stir in the feta with some salt and pepper. Leave it to cool slightly so you don't burn your fingers.

Make the pasta dough as per the instructions on page 16. Roll it out and cut out circles with a large cookie cutter.

Put a small amount of the filling on one half of the circle, leaving room around to seal it.

With a wet finger dab about the edge of the circle and fold it over. Seal it all the way around by gently pressing it together.

Repeat until the mixture or the dough is used up. It'll make plenty.

Put a large pan of salted water on to boil. You might have to cook the pasta in 2 batches.

Simmer for 3-5 minutes, then serve with a drizzle of olive oil, some pine nuts and Parmesan shavings.

HOW TO MAKE SIMPLE BREAD

Fancy artisan bread shops are all the rage at the moment, as people are taking more interest in where their food is coming from. Although the breads in these shops are delicious, they can be very expensive. You can use a bread proving basket, available from most cookware shops, to create a bread with a particular shape or pretty pattern (see photo), but it is not essential.

Makes 1 loaf or 6-8 rolls

Ingredients:
500g strong white flour,
plus extra for dusting
1 1/2 tsp salt
7g sachet fast-action yeast
3 tbsp olive oil
300ml cool water

Optional ingredients:
You could add 1-2 tbsp chopped olives, fruit, nuts or seeds to the dough during the folding process and before the first prove, or even roll it in sesame seeds or oats just before cooking

Mix the flour, salt and yeast in a large bowl, then make a well in the centre. Pour in the oil and water, and mix together. If the dough seems a little stiff, add 1-2 tbsp water.

Tip the dough onto a lightly floured work surface and knead it for 10-15 minutes or until it is satin smooth and stretchy.

Fold it in half four times, flip it over and place it in a large lightly oiled bowl. Cover with cling film and leave to rise in a warm place for at least 1 hour until doubled in size.

Then take it out and on a floured surface repeat the four times folding process. Do this three more times at 30 minute intervals, then place it in the basket (if you have one) and leave it to prove/rise for about 30 minutes. If you are making rolls, now is when you divide the dough. Shape it into 6-8 round balls and leave them to rise on a lightly covered tray.

Next, prepare for baking by preheating your oven to 230°C. Put a baking tray in to heat up and another tray at the bottom that will contain water to produce steam to aid the baking process. Put the kettle on to boil. Now transfer the loaf to the hot tray and slash the top with a serrated knife. You can spray it with water too if you want.

Put the baking tray back in the oven and pour a cup of boiling water into the bottom tray. Close the door quickly.

Bake the bread for 30-40 minutes or until it's golden brown and it sounds hollow when tapped underneath. It'll be 15-20 minutes for the rolls. Cool it on a wire rack.

GLUTEN-FREE BREAD

Not being able to eat fresh bread because you can't eat wheat must be so frustrating. I know there are many more gluten-free breads available in the supermarkets nowadays and not all of them taste like cardboard, but this recipe is so easy to make and works out cheaper too.

Makes 1 loaf

Ingredients:
2 egg whites
(or 20g chickpea flour and 60ml water)
1 tsp malt vinegar
2 tbsp sugar
2 tsp salt
400ml water
6 tbsp olive oil
500g gluten-free white flour,
plus extra for dusting
7g sachet fast-action yeast

Optional ingredients:
As you get better at making this loaf you could try adding 1-2 tbsp seeds such as pumpkin or sunflower to make it more interesting

Put the egg whites (or chickpea flour and water), vinegar, sugar, salt, water and half the oil in a large bowl and whisk.

Add the flour and yeast, and mix to a smooth paste.

Pour the rest of the oil over the dough and stir with a spoon, slowly bringing it all together.

Pour the dough into an oiled 1kg bread tin and spread it out evenly.

Cover it loosely with oiled clingfilm and leave it in a warm place to double in size. It should rise to the top of the tin in 30-45 minutes.

Preheat your oven to 200°C.

Carefully remove the clingfilm and bake the bread in the oven for 50-60 minutes or until it's golden and cooked through.

Tip it out and cool it on a wire rack.

EASY PIZZA DOUGH
and Margherita recipe

Everyone loves pizza, but buying them from the takeaway can be expensive. Why not make your own? This recipe really doesn't take long to make and works out so much cheaper; plus you can have it just the way you want it.

Makes 2 large pizzas

Ingredients for the pizza dough:
400g strong bread flour
100g fine semolina
1 tbsp fine sea salt
1 tsp easy-bake yeast
2 tsp caster sugar
300ml lukewarm water
1 tbsp oil

Ingredients for the sauce:
1 garlic clove, finely sliced
1 tbsp olive oil
Handful of fresh basil or 1 tsp dried
400g tin chopped tomatoes
Squirt of tomato purée
Salt and pepper to taste

Optional pizza toppings:
1 tbsp coarse semolina
2 big tomatoes, sliced
$\frac{1}{2}$ red onion, finely sliced
50g cheese, grated
125g mozzarella, sliced

To make gluten-free pizza:
See page 170

To make the pizza base, add water to the dry ingredients and mix well until a dough is formed. If it's too sticky, knead in a bit more flour. If it's too dry, add 1 tbsp more water.

Knead the dough for about 10 minutes until it's smooth and elastic, then pop it in a bowl and cover it with clingfilm. Set it aside in a warm place, ideally 30-40°C, for about 15 minutes.

Preheat the oven to 220°C.

While the dough is proving, make the tomato sauce. First cook the garlic gently in olive oil until it starts to turn golden. Next, add the basil, tomatoes, purée and a good pinch of salt and pepper and continue to fry on a low heat for a further 10 minutes. Then blend the sauce until it's smooth, have a little taste and season again if necessary.

Once the dough has risen a little, divide it into two balls. Roll out each ball on a flour-dusted surface to roughly 30cm in diameter and 3mm thick.

Place the pizza bases on lightly greased baking trays.

To make a crunchy crust, sprinkle some coarse semolina around the edges of the pizza.

Spread the sauce thinly over the base of the pizza, then add a sprinkle of cheese and your sliced ingredients, followed by the mozzarella. Season with salt and pepper.

Bake the pizzas in the oven for 10-15 minutes or until the cheese is melted and golden and the base is cooked.

BASIC CHAPATIS
or it could be a tortilla

Unleavened breads are a staple throughout the world and go by many different names. Here is one version that is extremely cheap and easy to make. We never buy chapatis from the supermarket any more as these taste so much better.

Makes 8 chapatis

Ingredients:
250g chapati (or plain) flour,
plus extra for dusting
(you can use gluten-free bread flour
instead with $\frac{1}{2}$ tsp xantham gum)
$\frac{1}{2}$ tsp salt
1 tbsp oil
150ml water

Sift the flour in a bowl with the salt and make a hole in the middle.

Pour in the oil and mix with a fork, then add the water and mix with your hands until you have a dough.

Leave the dough to prove for about 1 hour before rollng it out, if you have time.

On a flour-dusted surface, roll the dough with your hands into a long sausage and cut it into 8 equal slices. Then shape each one into a ball.

With a rolling pin, roll out each ball thinly to 20-25cm and place them on a plate with a dusting of flour between them.

In a dry frying pan, cook the chapatis on each side for about a minute, without browning them too much. Stack them and keep them warm in a low oven until they're needed.

HOW TO JOINT A CHICKEN
and save money

I don't know about you, but I never used to look too carefully at the prices of items as I was walking around the supermarket, so that I would receive a nasty surprise at the checkout when it came to much more than I was expecting. When I started looking into how much each item cost, I was amazed to find that 2 chicken fillets cost virtually the same as a whole chicken. I know it's more convenient to just pick up the filleted chicken breasts, but really that's such a waste. If you buy a whole chicken that's two fillets, two drumsticks, two thighs, two wings and a carcass for soup. Four meals instead of one.

These pages show you how you can make a chicken feed your family for more than just one meal, and save on food waste too.

I know it feels a bit unpleasant the first time you start cutting and filleting a chicken, but really it's not that bad once you get going; and at least the head and insides have been taken care of by the supermarket.

Be aware that raw chicken can contain Salmonella, so to be on the safe side make sure you have a bowl of hot soapy water ready to clean your hands when you've finished – you don't want to start turning on taps with chicken-contaminated hands. Also clean the area thoroughly afterwards.

Jointing a chicken should be done as soon as you bring it home from the supermarket. First take the legs off by pulling them away from the breast and cutting the skin at the joint to see the muscle. Cut down until you get to the bone, being careful not to cut into the breast fillet.

Next, fold back the leg so the joint pops out and you can see where to cut through to fully detach it. Once you have done this, you can start on the wings. Stretch out the wings so that you can feel where the bone joints meet the body, and cut through there.

Lastly, you'll need to take off the breast fillets. Feel with your finger where the breast bone is and start cutting with long strokes, removing the fillet close to the bone. Try not to hack it too much. Do the same with the other side.

You should now have the carcass, two legs which can be cut into thighs and drumsticks, two fillets and two wings. Bag up the pieces you don't need right away and either freeze them or keep them for a few days in the fridge. I save the wings in the freezer until I have enough to make a sticky barbecue meal (see page 122).

Remember you can reheat cooked chicken only once.

Although most of the recipes in this book contain cheaper cuts of chicken like the thighs and wings, when I have used breasts for my recipes, I've suggested frozen bags of them to keep within budget. But now you know how to joint a chicken, you could also use the breasts from a whole bird.

I used to turn my nose up at frozen foods, but since writing my blog I've realised that I end up freezing most of my meats anyway, so if it's cheaper to buy them ready-frozen it makes no difference. Just remember to defrost the chicken thoroughly before use, so that it cooks evenly.

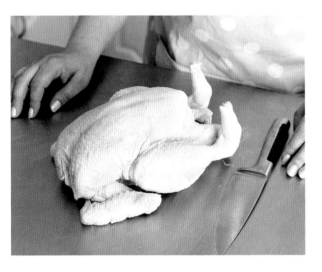
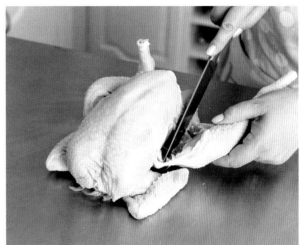
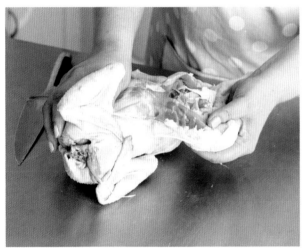

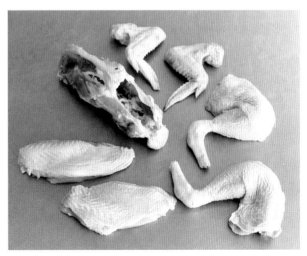

HOW TO MAKE STOCK

and save food waste

OK, so you've taken all the usable meat off the chicken and you're left with the carcass. Now what? Well, don't let it go to waste. You can make great chicken stock out of it. The advantage of making your own is that you will know it's gluten-free and doesn't contain loads of salt either.

You can freeze the stock in handy-size pots for a few months to use whenever you need them.

Firstly get your largest stock pot as you're going to need plenty of water here. I tend to save up the chicken carcasses in my freezer and cook a few of them at a time.

It may sound like I have a huge freezer, but I really don't. I just don't tend to have any shop-bought ready-meals filling it up.

Roughly chop a couple of celery stalks, a couple of carrots and a few white onions. Add a bay leaf or two if you have them, and a level teaspoonful of salt with a pinch of pepper. Once you have everything snugly in the pot, fill it with water to just cover the carcass. Bring it to the boil and then turn it down to a simmer for about 40-50 minutes.

Turn off the pan and let the stock cool a little, then pour it through a sieve into a large bowl, catching the mushy vegetables and chicken. You can throw the vegetables away if you're not using them to thicken soup but do pick the little bits of chicken off the carcasses to use in stir-frys, soups or even the Coronation Chicken (see page 86).

To make a vegetable stock use leeks, carrots, celery, onions, fennel and tarragon.

For a fish stock you can use the fish bones, skin, heads, prawn shells and heads as well as vegetables – just remember to strain it well. No one wants a fish eye floating in their soup.

HOT & SOUR CHICKEN SOUP

Serves 4

Ingredients:
1 litre home-made chicken stock
(see above)
1 tbsp soy sauce
1 tsp fresh grated or ground ginger
Juice of 1 lime
2 spring onions, finely sliced
1 chilli, finely chopped

Optional ingredients:
Leftover broken spaghetti or noodles
Bits of chicken picked off the stock carcass
Fresh coriander, to serve

Put the stock in a large saucepan.

Stir in the soy sauce, ginger and any other optional ingredients you have chosen. Bring the soup back to the boil and season it with the lime juice, salt and pepper.

Serve it hot with sliced spring onions, chopped chillies and coriander.

HOW TO MAKE SOUP

Soups are great to make from scratch as the shop-bought ones tend to be very high in salt and flavourings. The method for pretty much any vegetable soup is the same. Start by gently sautéing your vegetables in some oil, along with any dried herbs and spices. When they are soft and just starting to turn golden, pour in hot stock, or whatever liquid you are using, and bring the pan to the boil before turning it down to simmer for 10-20 minutes. When everything is cooked, whizz it up with a hand blender and season to taste.

Tomato Soup
1 tbsp olive oil
2 celery stalks, diced
1 medium carrot, diced
1 small onion, diced
1 garlic clove, finely chopped
400g tin chopped tomatoes
1 tbsp tomato purée
500ml vegetable stock (see page 31)
1 tsp mixed dried herbs

To serve:
1/2 chilli, deseeded and finely sliced
Dollop of natural yoghurt

Pea & Mint Soup
1 tbsp olive oil
2 celery stalks, diced
1 medium carrot, diced
1 medium onion, diced
1 litre vegetable stock (see page 31)
450g frozen peas

To serve:
Handful of fresh mint leaves

Carrot & Cumin Soup
2 tsp cumin seeds, dry fried
2 tbsp olive oil
600g carrots, grated
140g red lentils (or if green, soak for 30 minutes first)
1 litre vegetable stock (see page 31)
125ml milk

To serve:
1/2 chilli, deseeded and finely sliced
Fresh coriander, torn
Dollop of natural yoghurt

Black Bean Soup
1 tbsp olive oil
1/2 onion, chopped
1/2 red pepper, deseeded and chopped
1 celery stalk, chopped
1 chilli, deseeded and finely chopped
2 garlic cloves, sliced
1 1/2 tsp ground cumin
1 tsp ground coriander
1 bay leaf
400g tin chopped tomatoes
400g tin black beans, drained and rinsed
800ml chicken or vegetable stock (see page 31)

To serve:
Squeeze of lime juice
Dash of Tabasco
Spring onions, sliced
1/2 chilli, deseeded and finely sliced
Dollop of natural yoghurt

HOW TO MAKE SALAD DRESSINGS

Everyone knows we've all got to eat more salad and vegetables, but they can be so boring. Try jazzing yours up with these delicious salad dressings. Some of the ready-made ones can be very expensive, so making your own would be a great money-saving alternative. You can either mix the ingredients well in a bowl or give them a good shake in a clean jam jar.

Balsamic Dressing

6 tbsp extra-virgin olive oil
2 tbsp balsamic vinegar
Pinch of sea salt
Freshly ground black pepper
1 tsp lemon juice

Caesar-style Dressing

1 garlic clove, grated
4 tbsp natural yoghurt
2 tbsp capers, finely chopped
3 tbsp olive oil
Handful of freshly grated Parmesan cheese
2 tsp Worcestershire sauce
1 tsp lemon juice
Pinch of sea salt
Freshly ground black pepper

Honey & Mustard Dressing

6 tbsp extra-virgin olive oil
3 tbsp cider vinegar
1 tbsp Dijon mustard
1 tbsp honey
Pinch of sea salt
Freshly ground black pepper

Mint Yoghurt Dressing

1 garlic clove, grated
4 tbsp natural yoghurt
2 tbsp olive oil
Pinch of sea salt
Freshly ground black pepper
Handful of finely chopped mint

FILLED POTATO SKINS

Serves 4

Ingredients:
4 medium-sized potatoes
2-3 spring onions, finely sliced
1-2 tsp wholegrain mustard
Pinch of salt and pepper
150g Cheddar, grated

Optional ingredients:
A few chopped chives if you have them

Cook the potatoes in the oven at 200°C for 35-45 minutes or until they're soft when you squeeze them. You can start them off in a microwave to save time.

Carefully take them out and slice them in half to let them cool a little. Then scoop out the inside and mash it in a bowl with the onion, mustard and salt and pepper.

Place the skins open side up and cook them for a further 5 minutes. Meanwhile mix three-quarters of the cheese with the mashed potato in the bowl.

Take the hardened skins out of the oven and turn on the grill. Then fill each one with the mixture and top them with the rest of the grated cheese. Grill them for a few minutes until the cheese starts to melt and turn golden.

Garnish with a little sliced spring onion.

FLUFFY ROAST POTATOES

Serves 4

Ingredients:
4-5 large potatoes (Maris Piper or
King Edwards), peeled and quartered
Pinch of salt
2 tbsp olive oil

Optional ingredients:
500g parsnips, cut into batons

Preheat the oven to 200°C. Put the potatoes in a large saucepan of cold water with a pinch of salt and bring it to the boil, then turn down the heat and simmer for 4-5 minutes.

While the potatoes are cooking, pour the olive oil in a roasting tin and put it in the oven.

Drain the half-cooked potatoes in a colander, then return them to the saucepan and give them a little shake to dry them out and fluff up their edges. Not too hard — you don't want them to break up.

Now carefully tip the potatoes into the tray of hot oil. Turn each one to coat them in the hot oil, and return the tray to the oven. If you're cooking parsnips add them now too.

Roast them for 25-30 minutes, turning them once, until they're golden.

DAUPHINOISE POTATOES

Serves 4

Ingredients:
2-3 large potatoes (skins left on), thinly
sliced
$^1/_2$ red onion, thinly sliced
2 garlic cloves
100ml crème fraîche
100ml milk
2 handfuls of grated Parmesan or Cheddar
3-4 bay leaves
Few fresh thyme leaves if available
Drizzle of olive oil

Place the potatoes in a pan of boiling water for 3-4 minutes, then tip them into a colander to drain.

Next, place them in a large sturdy roasting tray and season them with salt and pepper. Crush in the garlic with the sliced onion, then pour in the crème fraîche and milk.

Sprinkle over half the cheese. Add the bay leaves, a few thyme leaves and a good drizzle of olive oil.

Mix everything together, scatter the rest of the cheese on top, then put the tray on the top shelf of the oven for 30-35 minutes, or until the surface is golden brown.

HOW TO MAKE AN ONION GRAVY
and other options

I will confess here that my husband is the best gravy maker I know, so these recipes are from him. You can use the meat juices from a roast as a base, and adjust all the ingredients to taste. Be creative; add a cup of apple juice for pork gravy, especially if roasting apples with the pork or a splash of orange juice if making gravy for duck.

Serves 4

Ingredients for onion gravy:
1-2 red onions, sliced into rings
1 tbsp cooking oil
1 tbsp plain flour
2 tsp wholegrain mustard
100ml red or white wine (optional)
1 stock cube dissolved in 600ml water
or 600ml home-made stock (see page 31)
Splash of Worcestershire sauce

Ingredients for mustard gravy:
2 tsp wholegrain or Dijon mustard
1 stock cube dissolved in 600ml water
or 600ml home-made stock (see page 31)
1 tbsp plain flour

Ingredients for gluten-free gravy:
600ml home-made stock (see page 31)
or 1 gluten-free stock cube dissolved in
600ml water
2 tbsp cornflour
50ml cold water

Sauté (gently fry) the onions in the oil for 10-15 minutes or until they're soft and caramelised.

Stir in the flour, then add the mustard, wine, stock and Worcestershire sauce and cook it off on a medium heat for about 10 minutes.

If it gets too thick add a little more hot water. If it's too thin simmer it for a little longer to reduce it. Season to taste.

If you are cooking a joint of meat, you can use the juices from it as a base for your gravy. With a tablespoon, skim off the fat and discard it (not down the sink). Using the same roasting tin on a high heat, stir in 600ml boiling water and scrape all the meat juices up from the bottom of the pan. Crumble in half a stock cube, a splash of Worcestershire sauce, the wine and mustard. Bring everything to the boil then reduce the heat and simmer until you have the right consistency.

If you're vegan, use vegan stock cubes or make your own vegetable stock – which can be frozen until needed (see page 31).

For a gluten-free gravy use 2 tbsp cornflour mixed in 50ml cold water instead of plain flour.

HOW TO MAKE A WHITE SAUCE
also known as béchamel

Knowing how to make a classic white sauce is a great cooking skill to master, as it's used in so many different recipes like lasagna, moussaka and parsley sauce for fish. I used to be scared of making it in case it went lumpy, but it's so easy, you'll never need to buy it ready-made again.

Serves 4

Ingredients for béchamel sauce:
50g butter
25g plain flour
600ml milk

Ingredients for parsley sauce:
50g butter
25g plain flour
600ml milk
Large bunch of parsley, finely chopped

Ingredients for cheese sauce:
50g butter
25g plain flour
600ml milk
100g grated cheese

Ingredients for vegan cheese sauce:
130g cashews
2 spring onions
2 tbsp yeast flakes
(from larger supermarkets and online)
$^1/_2$ tsp salt
250ml water

Ingredients for gluten-free béchamel sauce:
35g butter
800ml milk
25g cornflour or gluten-free plain flour

Melt the butter in a saucepan.

Stir in the flour and cook for 1-2 minutes.

Turn the heat down and gradually stir in the milk. This is the traditional French method. Alternatively, you can follow the method I was taught by an Italian chef: warm the milk up separately and then pour it all in at once and stir like crazy. The result will be the same.

Simmer gently for 8-10 minutes, stirring all the time with a spoon or balloon whisk, until the sauce is smooth, thick and creamy, and season with salt and pepper.

At this point you can add the cheese or parsley.

For the vegan cheese sauce, blend the nuts to a powder, then add the other dry ingredients, pouring the water in last. Blitz everything together, then transfer it to a saucepan and gently heat it until the sauce is thick and creamy.

For the gluten-free sauce, melt the butter then add the milk, followed by the cornflour, before simmering as before.

HOW TO MAKE SAGE & ONION STUFFING

We never buy the stuffing you get from a packet. It always tastes bland and thin. The good thing about making your own is that you can tailor it to your own tastes and dietary requirements, making it vegan or gluten-free. Plus it's a great way to use up leftover vegetables and breadcrumbs.

Makes 8 balls

Basic ingredients for stuffing:
1 large onion, finely chopped
1 tbsp oil
2 celery stalks, finely chopped
1 medium carrot, finely chopped
1 garlic clove, finely chopped
1 tsp dried herbs
120g breadcrumbs (made by blitzing / grating 3-4 stale crusts)
8-10 sages leaves, finely chopped
1 egg, beaten
1 tsp mustard

Optional ingredients:
120g mushrooms
Half a bunch of fresh parsley, chopped
8-10 apricots, chopped
Splash of red wine

Extra ingredients for Christmas stuffing:
Puréed and/or chopped chestnuts
Cranberries instead of apricots
Sausage meat
Extra sage

Vegan Christmas stuffing:
If serving vegans take out the egg and sausage meat, and make sure wine and bread is vegan

Preheat the oven to 200°C. Sweat your onions in the oil for 5 minutes, then add the celery and carrots and keep cooking for 5 more minutes until the veg has just started to soften and caramelise.

Now add the garlic, mushrooms and dried herbs and cook for another 10 minutes with a splash of red wine if you're using it.

Take the mixture off the heat and let it cool slightly while you mix together the other dry ingredients in a large bowl. Don't add all the breadcrumbs straight away; just use half.

Add the cooked onion mixture to your egg in another bowl and give it a good stir – it should be firm but not dry. Add a little boiled water if it's too dry or more breadcrumbs if it's too wet.

Divide the mixture into 8, roll it into balls and place them on an oiled baking sheet. Alternatively, spread the mixture across the bottom of a small lined loaf tin.

The balls will take about 20 minutes in the oven, and the loaf 25-30 minutes.

If you have any leftover cooked stuffing it is delicious in chicken sandwiches with a little mayonnaise.

To make the Christmas stuffing, prepare everything in the same way, omitting the mustard and adding the other ingredients to the mixture before rolling it into balls. Just make sure you double the quantities as people are going to want more.

We fill each end of the turkey with a different flavoured stuffing, factoring in extra cooking time accordingly.

BREADCRUMBED CHICKEN

Serves 4

Ingredients:
100g plain flour
2 eggs, beaten
Pinch of salt and pepper
100g breadcrumbs (see page 40)
4 chicken breasts

Optional ingredients:
You could zest a lemon and add it to the breadcrumbs with some chopped thyme leaves

Preheat the oven to 200°C.

Put the flour, the beaten eggs with salt and pepper, and the breadcrumbs into three separate bowls.

Dip the chicken breasts first in the flour, then in the egg and lastly in the breadcrumbs.

Pour some oil in a shallow pan and fry them for a few minutes on both sides, until the crumb goes a golden brown.

Then lay them on a baking tray and finish them off in the oven for about 10 minutes, and check they are cooked through.

Remove the chicken breasts and place them on some kitchen paper to absorb the excess oil.

POLENTA CHICKEN

Serves 4

Ingredients:
50g fine grain polenta or semolina
Pinch of salt and pepper
4 chicken breasts

Optional ingredients:
Add 1tsp either paprika, Cajun spice, cayenne pepper or cumin to pep it up a bit

Put the dry ingredients in a large bowl and give them a good stir.

Dip the chicken breasts in the mixture, turning them so they are coated evenly.

Pour some oil in a shallow pan and fry them for a few minutes on both sides, until the coating goes golden.

Then lay them on a baking tray and finish them off in the oven for about 10 minutes, checking they are cooked through.

Serve them sliced in a sandwich or with a salad for a main meal.

HOW TO MAKE SHORT-CRUST PASTRY
for a roasted vegetable quiche

The only pastry I have ever learnt how to make well is short-crust. It's a versatile, easy-to-use pastry. Sweeten it with a little icing sugar for mince pies, or use it for a savoury dish, like this quiche, without sugar. I never buy short-crust ready-made as it's not as nice. But I would always buy puff pastry, as that's such a faff to make.

Makes 8 slices

Ingredients for the pastry:
250g plain flour
Pinch of salt
130g cold butter, cubed
2-3 tbsp cold water
1 egg or milk to glaze

Ingredients for the filling:
1 red onion, roasted and sliced
1-2 peppers, roasted and sliced
150g Cheddar, grated
3-4 eggs
150ml single cream

Optional ingredients:
You can vary the ingredients depending on what you have left-over and needs using up – try different cheeses or ham or sprinkle in some dried herbs

To make the pastry case, put the flour and salt in a large bowl and add the cold cubes of butter.

Use your fingertips to rub the butter into the flour until you have a mixture that resembles coarse breadcrumbs with no large lumps of butter remaining. Try to keep the butter as cold as you can as this will make nicer pastry.

Using a fork, stir in just enough of the cold water to bind the dough together in a ball.

Wrap the dough in clingfilm and chill it in the fridge for at least 10-15 minutes.

After the pastry has chilled, pre-heat the oven to 180°C.

Roll out the pastry, then lay it with overhang for shrinkage in a 25cm loose-bottomed flan tin and blind bake it by putting some greaseproof paper on top and filling it with dried or ceramic beans. Put it in the oven for 10 minutes, then remove the beans and paper, cut the pastry edges flush and bake it for another 5 minutes.

While the pastry is cooking, make the quiche mixture by stirring the grated cheese into the beaten eggs and the cream. Season with a little salt and pepper.

When the pastry has had its 10 minutes, lay the roasted vegetables over the base then pour over the cheese and egg mixture.

Bake the quiche for 30-40 minutes, testing to see if it's set. Then leave it in the tin to cool and finish setting.

THE IMPORTANCE OF BREAKFAST
and home-made lunches

It's often said that breakfast is the most important meal of the day – well, I say they're all important, but having a good breakfast before you leave home in the morning can be an easy way to save money. I see plenty of people walking to work clutching an expensive coffee and pastry. How much did that cost? Wherever you buy them, you won't get much change from a fiver. That's £25 a week if you do it every day. One hundred pounds a month. A potential £1200 a year on a hot drink and sugary breakfast. Sure, every now and again is fine as a treat, but much better to have a proper breakfast of porridge and honey or toast and marmite, that should keep you going all morning and costs just pennies.

Now lunch – another time when people can spend a fortune, even with the 'meal deals'. I know we're not all ultra-organised and that making sandwiches takes time in the morning, but when you think about the money you could save, surely it's worth setting your alarm 10 minutes earlier? If you make your own breakfast and lunch you could be saving over £2000 every year on just these two meals.

The following few pages have alternative breakfast and lunch ideas that are made with leftovers or cheap ingredients from the shopping list provided.

I often go to work on a Monday morning with just a fiver in my purse and still have it on the Friday. It doesn't mean I don't have lovely food to eat, I'd just rather spend my money on other things.

MILKSHAKES

Milkshakes are a cheap way of getting berries or nuts into your diet. Peanut butter is a great source of protein, and dark purple and red berries are especially good for you. Best not to have them too often, though, as they both contain some sugars.

Serves 2

Ingredients for a peanut butter shake:
300ml milk
1 medium banana
1 heaped tbsp of peanut butter
1 tbsp honey or maple syrup

Ingredients for a summer berry shake:
300ml milk
1 medium banana
Large handful of frozen berries
1 tbsp honey or maple syrup

In a blender, blitz all ingredients for 30 seconds or until smooth.

Stir if necessary.

Pour into chilled glasses; serve immediately.

BUBBLE & SQUEAK

Serves 4

Ingredients:
At least 300g mashed potato
1 large or 2 small eggs, beaten
50g Cheddar, grated
150g leftover cabbage, peas, spinach
2 tbsp oil for cooking

Serve with:
Poached eggs

Optional ingredients:
1 tsp wholegrain mustard

Combine the mashed potato with the egg and cheese until you have a smooth mixture. Add the leftover vegetables with some salt and pepper.

Heat some oil in a frying pan. Make around 8 patties, using a heaped tablespoonful of the mixture for each, and fry them a few at a time over a medium heat.

Cook them for about 5 minutes on each side, then keep them warm in a low oven while you poach the eggs.

To poach an egg, keep a pan of water on a rolling boil, add a dash of vinegar and stir to create a whirlpool.

Crack the egg into a saucer and tip it into the whirlpool, then turn down the heat and poach it for about 3 minutes. Remove it with a slotted spoon. You could do 2 at a time with 2 pans to save time.

VEGAN PANCAKES

Serves 4

Ingredients:
100g oats
1 tsp baking powder
Pinch of sea salt
1 ripe banana, peeled and mashed
150ml vegan milk

Serve with:
Maple syrup and frozen berries

Mix all the ingredients together in a blender, then pour a little oil in a frying pan.

Place a tablespoonful of the mixture in a medium-hot pan. You can cook a few pancakes at a time, but make sure they're not touching. After a couple of minutes turn them over and cook the other side until they're golden brown.

Keep them warm until you want to serve them with the berries and maple syrup.

LEFTOVER WRAPS

Serves 4

Ingredients:
4 tortilla wraps
Leftover shredded meat
Fresh coriander
$1/2$ lettuce, shredded
1 carrot, grated
4 spring onions, sliced
Fresh chillies, sliced, to taste
Dollop of natural yoghurt for each tortilla

Lay out the tortilla wrap and pile on the rest of the ingredients, finishing with a dollop of natural yoghurt.

Fold in each end, then roll from the sides so that everything stays tucked inside.

Slice the tortilla in half and eat from the open end.

HOME-MADE HUMMUS & VEG

Serves 4

Ingredients:
200g canned chickpeas
2 tbsp lemon juice
1-2 garlic cloves, crushed
1 tsp ground cumin
Pinch of salt
1 tbsp tahini (sesame seed paste)
4 tbsp water
1 tbsp extra-virgin olive oil

Serve with:
Raw vegetables, such as carrots and
cucumber chopped into sticks
and toasted bread

If you can't get hold of tahini paste, leave it out. I have before and it's fine.

Drain and rinse the chickpeas. Reserve a few whole ones for serving.

Combine all the ingredients except the oil in a food processor and blend to a purée.

Add more lemon juice, cumin or salt to taste.

Drizzle a little oil over the hummus before serving.

CHICKEN QUESADILLA

Serves 4

Ingredients:
8 wraps
4 tsp sour cream, one for each quesadilla
Large handful of leftover chicken, chopped
2-3 spring onions, finely chopped
4 tbsp tinned sweetcorn
200g Cheddar, grated
$^1/_2$ bunch of coriander, roughly chopped

Serve with:
Pickled chillies or guacamole

Lay out 2 wraps at a time, and spread one with a teaspoonful of sour cream

Scatter the chicken, spring onions, sweetcorn, 50g Cheddar and some coriander on the other wrap, then place the sour cream wrap on top. Squish down a little.

Place the quesadilla in a dry frying pan over a medium heat for 3-4 minutes until it's just starting to brown and go crispy underneath.

Put a plate over the frying pan and turn the pan over to release the quesadilla, then slide the turned wrap back into the pan to cook the other side for 2-3 minutes.

You can place a smaller pan on top to weigh it down and help melt the cheese more quickly.

COLD PASTA SALAD

Ingredients:
Leftover cooked pasta
1 tbsp pesto
A few tomatoes, chopped
2 tbsp pine nuts
Shaved Parmesan
Handful of torn fresh basil leaves if you
have them

A tip when cooking extra pasta is to stir in a little olive oil to stop it sticking together. Then refrigerate once it's cold.

The next day for lunch, stir in the pesto, then mix in the other ingredients scattering the Parmesan and torn basil on top, along with a good grinding of black pepper.

WEEK 1

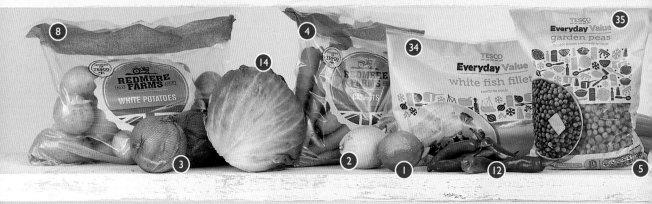

1	1 Lime	30p	**11**	1 Cucumber	50p
2	1 Lemon	30p	**12**	Mixed Chillies 65g	60p
3	Brown Onions 485g	65p	**13**	Ginger 50g	15p
4	Carrots 1kg	45p	**14**	2 Round/Iceberg Lettuce	80p
5	1 Garlic Bulb	30p	**15**	Cooking Peppers 600g	£1.10
6	2 Braeburn Apples	64p	**16**	2 Packets Salad Tomatoes 360g	£1.38
7	Red Onions 1kg	68p	**17**	British Unsalted Block Butter 250g	£1.09
8	White Potatoes 2.5kg	£1.29	**18**	Olive Oil Spread 500g	£1.00
9	Celery	55p	**19**	12 Medium Free Range Eggs	£1.75
10	2 Stems Thai Lemongrass	70p	**20**	British Milk 6 Pints	£1.48

21	Crème Fraîche 300ml	95p	
22	Cheddar Cheese 350g	£2.00	
23	Natural Yoghurt 500g	45p	
24	2 Value Sliced Wholemeal Bread 800g	80p	
25	Value Oats 1kg	75p	
26	Value Chopped Tomatoes 400g	31p	
27	Value Penne 500g	30p	
28	Value Strawberry Jam 454g	29p	
29	East End Desiccated Coconut 200g	£1.00	
30	Cocofresh Coconut Milk 400ml	75p	
31	3 Tins Value Tuna Chunks in Brine 160g	£1.95	
32	Tomato Puree Tube 200g	40p	
33	2 Packs British Chicken Thighs 1kg	£5.00	
34	Frozen Value White Fish Fillets 520g	£1.90	
35	Frozen Value Garden Peas 900g	69p	
36	Value Apple Juice 1 Litre	65p	
	Total	£33.90	

3 meals for a family of 4 × 7 days = £1.21 per person per day

MENU FOR WEEK 1
day-by-day

These week menu plans are designed to save you as much money as you can. They're designed around using the leftover ingredients from the shopping list as efficiently as possible. Although the food is budgeted tightly, feel free to try just a few of the recipes if you prefer. Check which stock cupboard ingredients you have run out of before you start.

    I haven't written out breakfasts for each day. But I have budgeted for simple and inexpensive daily rounds of toast and jam or porridge with maybe the odd egg at weekends. Week 1 has recipes that contain meat and fish, but there are menu plans for most dietary needs, including snacks and treats so you don't feel deprived.

Day 1
Lunch
Cheese on toast

Dinner
Tuna Salad Niçoise

Day 2
Lunch
Egg sandwiches

Dinner
Normandy Chicken with Dauphinoise potatoes

Day 3
Lunch
Cheese salad sandwiches

Dinner
Tomato & Tuna Pasta Bake

Day 4
Lunch
Cold pasta salad

Dinner
Coconut Chicken Curry

Day 5
Lunch
Tuna mayonnaise sandwiches

Dinner
All-in-one Baked Chicken with roasted vegetables

Day 6
Lunch
Chicken and mayo salad sandwiches

Dinner
Pasta Fritatta with mixed salad

Day 7
Lunch
Cheese salad sandwiches

Dinner
Fish & Chips with peas

Treat ideas
Easy Vanilla Biscuits
Coconut Slices
Flapjack

TUNA SALAD NIÇOISE
with Caesar-style dressing

This salad might not look like a lot, but you'll be surprised at how much there is once you start piling it up. It's very filling and, as you can see, it's packed with healthy protein to keep you feeling satisfied for longer.

Serves 4

Ingredients:
500g very small potatoes
3 eggs
2-3 crusts from your loaf of bread
$\frac{1}{2}$ iceberg lettuce, sliced
10cm cucumber, sliced into chunks
$\frac{1}{4}$ red onion, finely sliced
2 celery stalks, sliced
4 tomatoes, diced
A few olives (optional)
160g tin tuna, drained

To serve:
Caesar-style dressing (see page 35)

Boil the potatoes until they're soft but not mushy. Cool them in cold water, pat them dry, then slice them and arrange them on 4 plates.

Meanwhile, in a separate pan, hard-boil the eggs. This should take about 10 minutes. Then cool them by placing them under cold running water. When they're cold, peel them and cut them into wedges.

To make the croutons, cut up the bread crusts and fry them in a little olive oil with a pinch of salt.

Build up your salad by piling the chopped lettuce on top of the cooled potatoes, followed by the cucumber, onion, celery and tomatoes, then the olives, tuna and eggs, and lastly the croutons, all drizzled with the home-made Caesar-style dressing and some freshly ground pepper.

NORMANDY CHICKEN
with Dauphinoise potatoes

There are lots of different recipes for Normandy chicken and Dauphinoise potatoes, many passed down through French families. Traditionally cider or brandy are used, but I've opted for apple juice as it's cheaper. This Dauphinoise recipe is quick enough for midweek meals but would also be worthy of any dinner party.

Serves 4

Ingredients:
60g butter
4 skinless chicken thighs
2 brown onions
3 celery stalks, chopped
200ml apple juice (or cider)
300ml hot chicken stock
1 tbsp flour mixed to a paste with 2 tbsp water
100ml crème fraîche
2 apples, such as Braeburn, cored and cut into wedges
Handful of chopped fresh chives or parsley

To serve:
200g frozen peas
Dauphinoise potatoes (see page 37)

Optional ingredients:
If you don't have fresh herbs add some dried thyme while the dish is simmering

Heat half the butter in a roasting tin on the hob and brown the chicken thighs all over.

Add the onions and celery and cook for a few more minutes, then pour over the apple juice, stock and flour paste, season and mix well.

Bring it to the boil, then cover it with a lid and simmer for 25 minutes, or until the juices run clear from the chicken. Stir in the crème fraîche and simmer for 1 more minute.

While the chicken is cooking, heat the rest of the butter in a large frying pan and fry the apple wedges, until they're lightly coloured. When the chicken is ready stir in the apples and sprinkle some fresh chopped chives or parsley on top.

Serve with Dauphinoise Potatoes and cooked peas.

TOMATO & TUNA PASTA BAKE
with a mixed side salad

We all tend to cook too much pasta as we forget it expands when it's cooked, but it doesn't matter with this dish as the extra pasta will be used for a meal later in the week. I've used penne here as it's very cheap, but you could use other shapes or make your own if you prefer.

Serves 4

Ingredients for the pasta bake:
500g penne (save half of this for pasta fritatta, page 66)
1 tbsp olive oil
400g tin tomatoes, chopped
1 tbsp tomato purée
$\frac{1}{2}$ tsp fresh or dried oregano
2 garlic cloves, finely chopped
160g tin tuna, drained
Handful of grated Cheddar

Ingredients for the salad:
7-10cm cucumber, sliced into chunks
2-3 tomatoes, diced
$\frac{1}{4}$ red onion, thinly sliced
$\frac{1}{4}$ iceberg lettuce, sliced

Boil some salted water in a large pan and cook the pasta according to the packet instructions.

Meanwhile, start making the sauce. In a medium pan heat the oil, then tip in the tomatoes, tomato purée, herbs and garlic and a splash of water (or red wine). Simmer for around 10 minutes, or until the sauce has thickened.

Add half of the drained pasta to the sauce and stir in the tuna and some salt and pepper. Pour the mixture into an ovenproof dish, and scatter the cheese over the top.

Place the dish under the grill for a few minutes until the cheese has melted and turned golden. Serve the pasta bake with the salad on the side.

COCONUT CHICKEN CURRY
with chapatis

This curry recipe is quite mild even though it contains 3 chillies, as the coconut milk takes the heat out of it. Of course, you can add a bit more fire if you wish. If you like kormas, you're bound to love this. I've suggested chapatis as an accompanient to this meal but you can use rice instead.

Serves 4

Ingredients for the curry paste:
2 large brown onions, roughly chopped
8-10 garlic cloves
10cm root ginger, chopped
2 tsp ground turmeric
2 lemongrass stalks, outer leaves removed, soft inner stem chopped
2 fresh chillies, roughly chopped
2 tsp Chinese 5 spice powder
2 tbsp olive oil

Ingredients for the coconut curry:
6 tbsp desiccated coconut
2 tbsp cooking oil
4-6 chicken thighs, skinless
400ml tin coconut milk
$\frac{1}{2}$ tsp salt
1 tsp sugar
1 cinnamon stick
Juice of 1 lime

To serve:
Chapatis (see page 26)
Handful of fresh coriander
1 chilli, deseeded and finely sliced

First, blitz all the curry paste ingredients together in a food processor.

Then toast the desiccated coconut in a dry saucepan until lightly golden. The smell will tell you when it's ready. Prevent it from burning by constantly stirring it with a wooden spoon. Tip it into a bowl and set it aside.

Next, heat the oil in the same pan and cook the curry paste for 5 minutes.

Add the chicken and cook it for about 10 minutes, turning it frequently.

Stir in the coconut milk, salt, sugar and cinnamon stick and let it simmer with the lid on for 25-30 minutes, or until the chicken starts to fall off the bone.

At this point you can take the chicken thighs out and pull the meat off the bone. Put it back in once you have reduced the liquid a bit. Remember the sauce will thicken slightly when you add the desiccated coconut and the lime juice just before serving. Season to taste and scatter the coriander and sliced chilli, if using, on top.

Serve with the home-made chapatis.

PASTA FRITTATA
with mixed salad

This dish is a great way of using up leftover pasta which, if you cook it at the same time as the pasta bake (see page 63), will also save energy. You can add any other leftover ingredients to jazz it up a bit. Maybe some cooked bacon, rosemary or even spring onions.

Serves 4

Ingredients for the frittata:
5 eggs
80g Cheddar, grated
250g leftover cooked pasta
1 cup of frozen peas, defrosted
3 tbsp olive oil

Ingredients for the salad:
5cm cucumber, sliced into chunks
2 tomatoes, diced
1/4 red onion, thinly sliced
1/4 iceberg lettuce, sliced
1 carrot, thinly sliced

Preheat the oven to 200°C.

Beat the eggs in a large bowl, then add the grated cheese. Season with a little salt and a good twist of pepper. Whisk well, before stirring in the pasta and peas.

To cook the frittata, heat the oil in a large non-stick frying pan over a medium heat.

Add the egg mixture and cook it for about 5 minutes, or until it is crisp underneath, then carefully flip the frittata over onto a large plate, slide it back into the pan and return it to the hob for a further 5 minutes to cook the other side.

Serve it with a mixed salad. This frittata can be eaten hot or cold so is great for packed lunches and picnics.

ALL-IN-ONE BAKED CHICKEN
with roasted vegetables

This recipe is great for using cheaper cuts of chicken, but is still full of flavour as you cook the thighs with the skin on. The balsamic vinegar and paprika enhance the sweetness of the red onion. As this is a tray bake it's simple to cook; you just pop everything in a roasting tray and bung it in the oven.

Serves 4

Ingredients:
4 large ripe tomatoes
6 medium potatoes, washed
1 large red onion
2 red peppers
1 yellow pepper
4 chicken thighs, skin on
(Cook 2 more thighs for sandwiches)
4 garlic cloves
1 tsp paprika
2 tbsp cooking oil
2 tbsp balsamic vinegar
A few sprigs of fresh thyme or
½ tsp dried

To serve:
200g frozen peas

Preheat the oven to 180°C.

Quarter the tomatoes and the potatoes and place them in a large roasting tray.

Peel the onion and cut it into large wedges, then deseed and roughly chop the peppers.

Add all these to the tray, along with the chicken thighs.

Bash the unpeeled garlic cloves with the side of your knife and add them to the tray with the paprika, the oil, balsamic vinegar, herbs and a good pinch of salt and pepper.

Toss everything together and roast for around 40 minutes, or until the chicken is golden and cooked through and the potatoes are soft.

Serve with some cooked peas.

FISH & CHIPS
with peas & tartar sauce

When I was growing up, Friday night was always fish and chip night, but nowadays it can be quite expensive to buy a fish and chip supper for a family of four. So, feeling nostalgic for those earlier days, I've come up with a really cheap, home-cooked, healthier alternative, even including the peas and tartar sauce. All you need now is a jar of pickled eggs!

Serves 4

Ingredients for the fish:
4 frozen fish fillets
Crusts from 4 slices of bread
1 tsp lemon zest
2 tbsp olive oil
100g plain flour
1 egg, beaten with salt and pepper

Ingredients for the chips:
4 potatoes
1 tbsp fresh rosemary leaves, roughly chopped
1 tbsp olive oil

Ingredients for the tartar sauce:
100ml mayonnaise
2 tbsp capers, finely chopped
1 tbsp vinegar from the capers jar
2 tbsp gherkins, finely chopped
$1/2$ small onion, finely chopped
Squeeze of lemon juice
3 tbsp fresh parsley, chopped

To serve:
200g frozen peas
Lemon wedges

Defrost the fish fillets, and preheat the oven to 200°C.

Next, slice the potatoes into wedges and toss them in a tray with a little olive oil, a sprinkle of rosemary and a pinch of salt and pepper, then bake them in the oven for about 30 minutes.

Make your breadcrumbs by blitzing the crusts in a food processor or grating them. Then add the lemon zest, oil, salt and pepper and mix everything together.

Line up 3 shallow bowls: one with the flour, one with the beaten egg and one with the breadcrumbs.

Carefully roll the fish in the flour, followed by the egg mixture and then the breadcrumbs. Pat the mixture onto them if you need to.

Lay them side by side on lightly oiled greaseproof paper on a baking tray.

Bake them in the bottom of the oven for 12-15 minutes, carefully turning them halfway through.

To make the tartar sauce, mix together all of the ingredients with some pepper and salt in a small bowl. Taste it and adjust the ingredients to suit you.

Serve the fish with the cooked peas, the potato wedges and home-made tartar sauce.

WEEK 2

1	1 Lime	30p		**11**	1 Whole Cucumber	50p
2	1 Lemon	30p		**12**	2 Bunches of Fresh Coriander	£1.40
3	1 Cabbage	49p		**13**	2 Round/Iceberg Lettuces	80p
4	Carrots 1kg	45p		**14**	Cooking Peppers 600g	£1.10
5	1 Garlic Bulb	30p		**15**	Bunched Spring Onions 100g	49p
6	Closed Cup Mushrooms 300g	79p		**16**	2 Packets Salad Tomatoes 360g	£1.38
7	Red Onions 1kg	68p		**17**	1 Chilli	12p
8	White Potatoes 2.5kg	£1.29		**18**	British Unsalted Block Butter 250g	£1.09
9	Baby Potatoes 1kg	89p		**19**	Olive Oil Spread 500g	£1.00
10	1 Avocado	60p		**20**	Half Fat Crème Fraîche 300ml	95p

21	British Milk 6 Pints	£1.48	31	Sharwoods Mango Chutney 227g	79p
22	Jus Rol Puff Pastry Ready Rolled 320g	£1.00	32	Value Spaghetti 500g	20p
23	Natural Yoghurt 500g	45p	33	Value Strawberry Jam 454g	29p
24	Cheddar Cheese 350g	£2.00	34	12 Free Range Eggs	£1.75
25	Value Sliced White Bread 800g	40p	35	Pork Shoulder Joint 2kg	£5.18
26	2 Value Sliced Wholemeal Bread 800g	80p	36	Frozen Chicken Breast Fillets 1kg	£3.82
27	Value Tin Sweetcorn 325g	35p	37	Frozen Garden Peas 900g	69p
28	Value Oats 1kg	75p		Total	£35.58
29	Value Chopped Tomatoes 400g	31p			
30	Tomato Purée Tube 200g	40p			

3 meals for a family of 4 x 7 days = £1.27 per person per day

MENU FOR WEEK 2
day-by-day

Week 2 again has meat and fish. This time I have even included pulled pork, although if you don't eat pork you could replace it with lamb or beef done in the slow cooker. While the budget is very tight, I still only buy eggs that are free range.

These shopping lists don't contain a lot of fruit but there are plenty of vegetables and salad to help you maintain a balanced diet. If you want to add more fruit go ahead, but do remember that it can contain a lot of natural sugars so you shouldn't have more than 2 portions a day.

Day 1
Lunch
Tomato soup with cheese sandwiches

Dinner
Chicken Caesar-style Salad

Day 2
Lunch
Breaded chicken salad sandwiches

Dinner
Slow-cooked Pulled Pork with roast potatoes, carrots and cabbage and baked apples

Day 3
Lunch
Pulled pork and salad wraps or sandwiches

Dinner
Sweetcorn Fritters with spicy salad and mango chutney

Day 4
Lunch
Cheese salad sandwiches

Dinner
Carbonara-style Pasta

Day 5
Lunch
Cold pasta salad

Dinner
Chicken & Mushroom Pie with mashed potatoes and peas

Day 6
Lunch
Egg sandwiches

Dinner
Coronation Chicken with Indian spiced potatoes

Day 7
Lunch
Coronation chicken sandwiches

Dinner
Mushroom Omelette, potato wedges and salad

Treat ideas
Moravian Sugar Cake
Easy Vanilla Biscuits
Flapjack

CHICKEN CAESAR-STYLE SALAD

This is a great simple salad recipe, full of flavour and goodness. It's made in the style of the famous Caesar salad invented in Vegas, but with much cheaper ingredients so anyone can enjoy it, not just the high rollers.

Serves 4

Ingredients:
3-4 chicken breasts
Handful of flour
1 egg, beaten
100g breadcrumbs (see page 40)
2 slices of bread, for croutons
3 tbsp olive oil
$1/2$ iceberg lettuce, sliced
10cm cucumber, sliced into chunks
2 carrots, thinly sliced
1 pepper, deseeded and diced
2 spring onions, sliced
4 tomatoes, diced

To serve:
Caeser-style dressing (see page 35)

Lay the chicken breasts on a chopping board between 2 sheets of brown parchment paper and with a rolling pin hit them quite hard to flatten them out a bit (about 1cm thick).

Line up 3 separate bowls: one with flour, one with the egg and one with breadcrumbs and some pepper and salt. Dip the chicken breasts in the flour, then in the egg and lastly in the breadcrumbs.

Heat some oil in a shallow pan and fry the chicken breast for a few minutes on each side, until the crumb coating goes a golden brown. You can cut one in half to make sure it is cooked through.

Remove the chicken and place it on some kitchen paper to absorb the excess oil. Slice it thinly to make it go further, and save one breast for sandwiches.

To make the croutons preheat the oven to 180°C. Cut the bread slices into cubes and toss them in a bowl with 2 tbsp olive oil. Sprinkle a pinch of salt over them and bake them on a tray for about 15 minutes or until they're golden and crisp.

Now build up your salad by piling the chopped lettuce on the plate followed by the cucumber, carrots, pepper, spring onion and tomatoes, then the sliced breaded chicken and lastly the croutons. Drizzle the home-made Caesar-style dressing on top with some freshly ground pepper.

SLOW-COOKED PULLED PORK

Slow-cooking is a great way to get the best out of cheaper cuts of meat which become tenderised by being exposed to a low heat over time. Cooking in a slow cooker or crock-pot is fuel-efficient, too. This recipe would work just as well with a shoulder of lamb.

Serves 4 with leftovers for other meals

Ingredients:
4 tbsp soy sauce
2 tbsp brown sugar
1 tbsp Worcestershire sauce
1 tbsp white wine vinegar
2 tsp paprika
1 tsp cayenne pepper
2kg shoulder of pork

Serve with:
2 baked apples (half each)
Roast potatoes
Carrots
Cabbage and peas

In a large bowl, mix all the marinade ingredients together.

Cut the skin off the pork to use for crackling later and put the joint in the bowl, making sure it's well coated in the marinade. Cover it and leave it in the fridge overnight. Put the skin in the fridge too.

In the morning, place the pork and marinade in a slow cooker and cook it on a low setting for 6-7 hours.

If you're using a conventional oven, cook it for about 3 hours at 140°C in a roasting tray covered with foil.

About 40 minutes before the meat is ready to come out, turn up the oven to 200°C.

Now lay the pork skin on a board and with a sharp knife make deep scores along the surface about 1cm apart. Rub some salt into the skin and roast it in the oven with the potatoes (see recipe on page 37).

To bake the apples, simply score a line around the middle to stop them exploding in the oven and cook them for about 30 minutes. This can be done at the same time as the roast potatoes and crackling. (You could also roast a couple of peppers while the oven is on as they can be used later in the week.)

Once the pork is cooked, remove any fat and pull the meat apart with forks.

You can make a gravy using a little of the meat juices (see page 38).

SWEETCORN FRITTERS
With spicy salad and mango chutney

This light, Asian-inspired supper is full of colour and zest, perfect for a summer evening or to cheer up a grey day. The soft, creamy texture of the avocado works well with the crunchy sweetcorn fritters and spicy salad.

Serves 4

Ingredients for the salad:
2 tbsp oil
1 tsp black/yellow mustard seeds
2 roasted red peppers
1 large carrot, grated
1 large red onion, finely chopped
1/4 bunch of fresh coriander, roughly chopped
Juice of 1/2 lime

Ingredients for the fritters:
200g tin sweetcorn
2 medium onions
1 egg
60g plain flour
1/2 bunch fresh coriander
Zest of 1/2 lime
1 tsp ground cumin
1 tsp chilli powder
1/2 chilli, deseeded
1 tsp salt
Pinch of pepper
2 tbsp oil for frying

To serve:
Mango chutney
Lime wedges
1 avocado
1/2 chilli, deseeded finely chopped

Optional ingredients:
Lettuce leaves for the salad

To make the salad, heat the oil and fry the mustard seeds in a small frying pan for about a minute until they start popping. Pour the seeds and oil into a bowl and set them aside.

Cut the roasted peppers into strips and toss them in a bowl with the other salad vegetables and the coriander.

To make the fritters, put all the fritter ingredients in a food processor, except for a few of the sweetcorn kernels which you can add to the salad to give it more texture. Blitz everything together – the mixture should still be a bit chunky.

Put some oil in a frying pan over a medium-high heat.

Scoop 1 heaped tablespoonful of the batter into the frying pan, flattening it slightly to create a patty shape, and fry it for a few minutes on each side until it is golden brown and cooked through. You can probably cook a couple at a time, then drain them on kitchen paper and keep them warm in a low oven until they're all cooked.

Finish the salad by stirring in the mustard seeds and oil along with the lime juice with a pinch of salt and pepper to taste.

Serve the fritters with lime wedges, some mango chutney, slices of avocado and the salad and the chopped chilli scattered over.

CARBONARA-STYLE PASTA
with pulled pork & mushrooms

Carbonara is the ultimate comfort food. This creamy sauce doesn't pretend to be a traditional carbonara, but I was taught how to make it by an Italian cook so it has some claim to authenticity. Using the leftover pulled pork gives it a mild spicy flavour that really lifts it from an ordinary carbonara. You can use the opportunity to cook some extra pasta for lunches in the week.

Serves 4

Ingredients for the carbonara:
300g spaghetti
Knob of butter
1 tbsp oil
100g mushrooms, sliced
90g Cheddar, finely grated
2 tbsp crème fraîche
2 eggs
Salt and pepper
100g frozen peas
150g leftover pulled pork

Ingredients for the salad:
4cm cucumber, sliced into chunks
2 tomatoes, diced
1/4 iceberg lettuce, sliced
1/2 red pepper, sliced

Optional ingredients:
Parmesan instead of Cheddar
This would work well with leftover chicken or turkey too

Cook the pasta according to the packet instructions.

Meanwhile melt the butter and oil in a deep-sided frying pan and gently fry the mushrooms for a few minutes.

Beat the cheese, crème fraîche and eggs in a bowl with a fork, season with salt and pepper.

Add the peas and pork to the mushrooms and cook for a few more minutes until everything is heated through.

When the spaghetti is ready, drain it over a bowl, keeping back a little of the starchy water, then stir it into the pork and mushroom mixture.

Turn off the pan and pour in the egg mixture, tossing well to combine – you don't want the eggs to scramble, but you do want them to cook in the heat of the pasta.

If it's a bit dry, add a little of the saved water to loosen it slightly.

Serve immediately with more ground pepper, some cheese to taste and the salad.

CHICKEN & MUSHROOM PIE
with mashed potato and minted peas

This is a little bit of English tradition on a plate. I love the combination of mustard and thyme that flavour the sauce and with the mushy peas and mashed potato you could be in a classy East End pie shop. Make sure you make some extra mash to save for a cake recipe later in the week (see recipe on page 194).

Serves 4

Ingredients for the pie:
1 tbsp olive oil
Knob of butter
1 onion, finely chopped
3 chicken breasts, cut into bite-size pieces
2 garlic cloves, finely chopped
100g mushrooms, sliced
1 heaped tsp plain flour (plus extra for dusting)
2 tsp English mustard
1 tbsp crème fraîche
300ml chicken stock (see page 31 for homemade recipe)
2 tsp fresh thyme leaves, finely chopped or 1 tsp dried
100g frozen peas, defrosted
Sea salt and pepper
1/2 packet of puff/flaky pastry, rolled out (the other 1/2 can be frozen for another day)
1 egg, for glazing

Ingredients for the mash:
4 large potatoes, peeled and quartered
Knob of butter
25ml milk

Ingredients for the peas:
1/4 onion, finely chopped
25g butter
550g frozen peas
125ml vegetable stock
Small handful of fresh mint leaves

Pre-heat the oven to 200°C.

Place the olive oil and butter in a large pan over a medium heat, soften the onions and then add the chicken and garlic and fry them gently until they're golden – about 5 minutes.

Add the mushrooms and the flour to the pan and give it all a good stir. Mix in the mustard, crème fraîche and chicken stock.

Next, add the thyme and some peas and season with sea salt and pepper. Leave the sauce to simmer and thicken while you roll out your pastry on a floured work surface to a size slightly bigger than your baking dish.

Once your chicken filling has thickened up, tip it into the dish. Cover it with the sheet of pastry, tucking the edges in roughly around the dish, glaze the top with the beaten egg.

Bake it for 25-30 minutes or until the pastry is golden.

Meanwhile, make the mash by boiling the potatoes in a large saucepan, drain them when they are soft and with a masher beat in the butter, milk and some seasoning until it is a smooth consistency.

To make the mushy peas, soften the onions with butter in a saucepan. Add the peas and stock and bring it to the boil, then reduce the heat and simmer for 5 minutes.

Stir in the mint and cook for a few more minutes. Spoon the mixture into a food processor and blend until you have the consistency you like and season to taste.

CORONATION CHICKEN WITH INDIAN SPICED POTATOES

Coronation chicken was invented to celebrate Queens Elizabeth's coronation in 1953, using ingredients from around the Commonwealth. This recipe is a cheat's version that can be knocked up in minutes. It works really well with the spicy new potatoes and chapatis. You can make it as mild or as spicy as you like.

Serves 4

Ingredients for the spicy potatoes:
800g baby potatoes
Olive oil
2 tsp cumin seeds
1 tbsp ground turmeric
2 spring onions, finely sliced
1 lemon (or 1 tbsp lemon juice)
2 tbsp mixed seeds, such as pumpkin and sunflower seeds
$1/2$ bunch of fresh parsley
150g cooked peas, cooled
1 tsp chilli flakes

Ingredients for the chicken:
2-3 chicken breasts
2 tbsp mayonnaise
1 tbsp natural yoghurt
1 tbsp mango chutney
1 tsp mild curry powder
Handful of fresh coriander, chopped(optional)

To serve:
Small bowl of natural yoghurt sprinkled with chopped fresh coriander
Chapatis (see page 26)

Preheat the oven to 190°C. Bring a large pan of salted water to the boil.

Leaving the skins on, halve any larger potatoes, then place them all in the water and parboil them for 8-10 minutes.

Drain them, then transfer them to a roasting tray and toss them in the oil, cumin seeds, turmeric and some seasoning. Roast them in the oven for 20-25 minutes.

Place the spring onions in a shallow bowl, squeeze over the lemon juice and leave them to soak.

Toast the seeds in a dry pan and set them aside. Pick and finely chop the parsley leaves.

When the potatoes are ready, leave them to cool a little, then transfer them to a serving bowl. Add the onions, parsley, cooked peas and a drizzle of oil and toss everything together, then sprinkle the toasted seeds on top.

For the coronation chicken, place the chicken breasts in a pan of cold water and bring it to the boil. Cover the pan, reduce the heat and leave to simmer for around 15 minutes or until the chicken is cooked through. Remove it from the pan and let it cool before shredding it with 2 forks.

Mix it with the mayonnaise, yoghurt, mango chutney and a sprinkling of mild curry powder. Season well and stir in some chopped coriander.

Serve with chapatis and yoghurt.

MUSHROOM OMELETTE
with potato wedges & salad

Omelettes are fantastically versatile, great for using up leftover ingredients, like tomatoes, mushrooms, ham or cheese. Using a grill briefly at the end to cook the top is a good trick when making one big omelette, as it would be a messy job to flip it in the pan.

Serves 4

Ingredients for the omelette:
2 tbsp oil
100g mushrooms, thinly sliced
Sprig of thyme, leaves only
6-7 eggs
Knob of butter
Salt and pepper
50g Cheddar, grated

Ingredients for the salad:
4cm cucumber, sliced into chunks
2 tomatoes, diced
2 spring onions, sliced
1/4 iceberg lettuce, sliced
1 carrot, thinly sliced
1 red pepper, diced

To serve:
Rosemary potato wedges (see page 70)

Optional ingredients:
As this is the last day of the week you can add any spare peppers or tomatoes to the omelette with the mushrooms

First off, get your potato wedges in the oven, and then prepare the salad and set it aside.

Heat an ovenproof frying pan with the oil and add the sliced mushrooms with the thyme leaves. Gently fry them for about 10 minutes.

Meanwhile, crack the eggs into a bowl and add the butter, salt and pepper and beat well with a fork.

Add the eggs to the mushrooms and gently stir in the sides of the mixture to the centre as it begins to cook. After a couple of minutes, scatter over the cheese.

To cook the top of the omelette, place the frying pan under a hot grill for a few minutes until it's golden and bubbling and the cheese has melted.

Serve it with the salad and potato wedges.

WEEK 3

1	Bananas 5 Pack	80p	**11**	1 Cucumber	50p
2	1 Lime	30p	**12**	2 Bunches of Fresh Coriander	£1.40
3	Ginger 50g	15p	**13**	Mixed Chillies 65g	60p
4	Carrots 1kg	45p	**14**	Round/Iceberg Lettuce	40p
5	1 Garlic Bulb	30p	**15**	Cooking Peppers 600g	£1.10
6	2 Aubergines	£1.20	**16**	Packet Salad Tomatoes 360g	69p
7	Red Onions 1kg	69p	**17**	Chestnut Mushrooms 260g	79p
8	Brown/White Onions 485g	65p	**18**	British Unsalted Block Butter 250g	£1.09
9	White Potatoes 2.5kg	£1.29	**19**	1 Avocado	90p
10	Celery	55p	**20**	6 Mixed Sized Free Range Eggs	89p

21	British Milk 6 Pints	£1.48		31	Lentils 500g	£1.15
22	Cheddar Cheese 350g	£2.50		32	Wholefood Black Turtle Beans 500g	£1.80
23	Value Feta Cheese 200g	75p		33	6 Tins Value Chopped Tomatoes 400g	£1.86
24	Natural Yoghurt 500g	45p		34	Tomato Purée Tube 200g	40p
25	2 Value Sliced Wholemeal Bread 800g	80p		35	Value Spaghetti 500g	20p
26	4 Brioche Burger Rolls	90p		36	Value Crunchy Peanut Butter 340g	65p
27	Value Oats 1kg	75p		37	Olive Oil Spread 500g	£1.00
28	Packet Value Tortilla Chips 200g	46p			Total	£31.44
29	Value Strawberry Jam 454g	29p				
30	2 Tins Value Dark Red Kidney Beans 400g	60p				

3 meals for a family of 4 x 7 days = £1.12 per person per day

MENU FOR WEEK 3
day-by-day vegetarian

Eating vegetarian is a brilliant way of cutting down the costs on your shopping budget. Plus it is suprisingly easy to skip meat when you cook dishes with plenty of interesting flavours. And this week's recipes definitely don't scrimp on taste; from India to Mexico to the Mediterranean, there are flavours from a wide range of cuisines.

It is important when following a vegetarian diet to remember to maintain a healthy balance of nutrients. I have added peanut butter and different kinds of beans and pulses to the shopping list as they are good sources of protein while also doing a great job of making you feel full.

Day 1
Lunch
Mushrooms or cheese on toast

Dinner
Aubergine Curry with pakoras and chapatis

Day 2
Lunch
Black bean soup or cheese sandwiches

Dinner
Lentil 'Shepherds' Pie with carrots and cabbage

Day 3
Lunch
Cheese salad sandwiches or leftover shepherds pie

Dinner
Amazing Veggie Burger with chips and salad

Day 4
Lunch
Cheese sandwiches

Dinner
Greek Potatoes Yiachni

Day 5
Lunch
Egg sandwiches

Dinner
Black Bean Tacos with guacamole and salsa salad

Day 6
Lunch
Lentil soup or cheese sandwiches

Dinner
Mediterranean Spiced Pasta

Day 7
Lunch
Cold pasta salad

Dinner
Veggie Chilli with cheesy nachos

Treat ideas
Flapjack
Banana Bread
Orange Loaf Cake
Peanut and Banana Milkshake

AUBERGINE CURRY
with pakoras & chapatis

This vegetarian curry is bursting with flavour and healthy ingredients. Add more spice if you like it fiery. The pakoras are very easy to assemble but take care not to splash yourself with hot spitting oil when frying them.

Serves 4 (with leftover pakoras for lunches)

Ingredients for the curry:
2 aubergines, thinly sliced
3 tbsp oil
2 tsp black mustard seeds
2 tsp fennel seeds
2.5cm root ginger, grated
4 garlic cloves, crushed
1 tsp ground turmeric
1 tsp curry power
2 tbsp garam masala
3 tsp ground coriander
1 1/2 tins chopped tomatoes
1 tbsp tomato purée

Ingredients for the pakoras:
250g plain flour
1 tsp cumin seeds
1 tsp salt
1/2 tsp curry powder
1 tsp ground coriander
1/2 tsp bicarbonate of soda
2 tsp garam masala
1 chilli, finely chopped
2 medium onions, thinly sliced
1 carrot, grated (or any other leftover vegetables)
100ml cold water
Vegetable oil for frying

To serve:
Handful of fresh coriander, chopped
Dollop of natural yoghurt
Chapatis (see page 26)

Heat some oil in a frying pan and fry the aubergine slices a few at a time until they're slightly brown on both sides, then set them aside.

Preheat the oven to 160°C to keep the pakoras warm.

In a deep saucepan, heat 1 tbsp oil and gently fry the mustard and fennel seeds. Once they start to pop, add the ginger, garlic and other spices, and stir for a minute or two.

Then add the tinned tomatoes, 75ml water and the tomato purée. Cook the sauce on a medium heat for 10 minutes or until it's slightly thickened, then season to taste. Add the aubergines, reduce the heat and simmer for another 10 minutes. Don't stir too much as you don't want to break them up.

While the curry cooks, make the pakoras. Mix all the dry ingredients together in a large bowl, then add the vegetables with the water and stir well so everything is combined.

Heat 2cm oil in a deep frying pan and gently drop in a tablespoonful of the mixture. You can cook a few at a time. Flattening the pakoras will help them cook a little faster.

When they turn golden, remove them with a slotted spoon and keep them warm in the oven while you finish the others and the curry. You'll end up making 25-30 pakoras.

Serve the curry with some natural yoghurt and a scatter of chopped coriander.

UNDER
£3
FOR FOUR

LENTIL 'SHEPHERD'S' PIE
with carrots & cabbage

This vegetarian shepherd's pie is just as satisfying as the meat version. If you can make the filling in advance, do. It often tastes better if it has been made a day before as the flavour has had time to mature. It is not necessary to soak lentils before cooking but it does reduce the cooking time.

Serves 4 (plus lots for leftovers)

Ingredients:
250g dried green lentils
25g butter
1 onion, chopped
2 carrots, diced
2 garlic cloves, finely chopped
2 bay leaves
100g chestnut mushrooms, sliced
1 tbsp fresh thyme leaves or $\frac{1}{2}$ tbsp dried
1 tbsp tomato purée
50ml red wine (optional)
800ml vegetable stock
5-6 large potatoes
Dash of oil
Pinch of salt and pepper
50g cheese, grated (optional)

To serve:
Carrots, cabbage or peas

Soak the lentils in cold water for 30 minutes to soften them.

Heat the butter in a pan, and gently fry the onions, carrots and garlic for 15 minutes or until they're soft and golden. Turn up the heat, add the bay leaves and mushrooms and cook for 4 minutes more.

Add the drained lentils and thyme, then stir in the tomato purée. Pour in the wine and stock and mix it all together – it's important that you do not season with salt at this stage or the lentils will go hard.

Simmer for 40-50 minutes or until the lentils are very soft.

Ten minutes before the end of the cooking time, remove the lid to reduce the liquid, then season to taste.

Preheat the oven to 190°C.

While the lentils are cooking, peel and dice the potatoes and place them in a pan of salted water. Bring it to the boil, then simmer for about 15 minutes or until they're soft. Drain them and return them to the pan with a little oil, salt and pepper and mash them until they're smooth.

To assemble the pie, put the lentil sauce in a deep casserole, cover it evenly with the mashed potato, roughen the surface with a fork and sprinkle the cheese on top. Bake it for 20-30 minutes or until the top is golden and crisp.

Serve with carrots and cabbage.

AMAZING VEGGIE BURGER
with chips & salad

This lightly spiced patty makes a delicious veggie burger. It is hearty, filling and healthy, packed with protein. The sauce is a traditional Marie-Rose which is very simple to make. Worcestershire sauce contains anchovies so I have suggested mushroom sauce as a vegetarian alternative.

Serves 4

Ingredients for the veggie patty:
400g tin kidney beans, drained and rinsed
1 small onion, finely chopped
1 large carrot, grated
1 tsp ground cumin
1 tbsp oil
1 tsp cayenne pepper
1 heaped tsp flour
4 slices of Cheddar

Ingredients for the Marie-Rose sauce:
2 tbsp each ketchup and mayonnaise
Splash of Worcestershire sauce (or mushroom sauce)
Dash of lemon juice

Ingredients for the burger bun:
$^1/_4$ red onion, thinly sliced
Iceberg lettuce, sliced
4 brioche burger rolls
Gherkins, sliced (optional)

Ingredients for the salad:
$^1/_4$ cucumber, diced
2 tomatoes, diced
$^1/_4$ red onion, thinly sliced
$^1/_4$ iceberg lettuce, sliced
1 carrot, thinly sliced
1 pepper, deseeded and thinly sliced

To serve:
Rosemary potato wedges (see page 70)

Put the kidney beans in a saucepan and cover them with cold water. Bring it to the boil, then reduce the heat and let them simmer for 10 minutes. Drain them and set them aside.

Meanwhile, soften the onion, carrot and cumin in a splash of oil in a medium frying pan on a low heat. Pour in the drained beans and cayenne pepper and cook for another 5 minutes or so.

Remove the pan from the heat and mash until you have a smooth purée, stirring in the flour to bind the mixture. Leave it to cool for a few minutes while you whisk all the sauce ingredients together in a bowl.

Divide the burger mixture into 4 and roll it into balls. Heat the remaining oil in a frying pan and gently fry the patties over a medium heat, flattening them to make a burger shape and turning them after a few minutes. You need to be gentle as they can be quite fragile before they are fully cooked.

When you've fried both sides, put a slice of cheese on top of each one and cover the pan for a minute or so until the cheese starts to soften.

Meanwhile, assemble the salad and prepare the buns by slicing them in half and lightly toasting the insides. Then spread a layer of sauce on one half and place the lettuce and burger on top, followed by the onions and the gherkins, and finally the other half of the bun.

Serve them with potato wedges and salad.

GREEK POTATOES YIACHNI
with feta, salad & tzatziki

This dish reminds me of that long-ago childhood Greek holiday, going into a restaurant and not knowing what we were ordering. I still can't pronounce this dish, but it's delicious anyway. The red onions in the salad are sweet enough to eat raw and work well with the feta cheese.

Serves 4

Ingredients for the potatoes:
600g potatoes
4 tbsp olive oil, plus extra to serve
2 medium onion, finely sliced
1 tsp dried oregano, plus extra to serve
3 garlic cloves, crushed
1 1/2 tin chopped tomatoes
3 fresh bay leaves
1 cinnamon stick
Handful of olives (optional)
150g Feta or salad cheese

Ingredients for the salad:
1 red onion, finely sliced
1/2 cucumber, sliced
2 tomatoes, cut into chunks
Handful of olives
50g Feta or salad cheese, cut into chunks
Drizzle of olive oil

Ingredients for the tzatziki:
1/4 cucumber
3 tbsp Greek or natural yoghurt
2 garlic cloves, crushed
1 tbsp olive oil
Few drops of lemon juice
Handful of fresh mint leaves,
finely chopped

Peel the potatoes if they're not new and cut them into quarters.

Heat the oil in a large saucepan or deep frying pan and sauté the onions, oregano and garlic for 5 minutes. Season with salt and pepper.

Add the potatoes, tomatoes, bay leaves and cinnamon to the pan and stir well. Pour in enough boiling water to just cover the mixture, put the lid on and simmer on a low heat for about 30 minutes.

Remove the lid, add the olives and continue to cook, stirring occasionally, for a further 10 minutes, or until the sauce has thickened and the potatoes are tender.

Crumble the Feta cheese over the dish along with a sprinkling of oregano and a good drizzle of extra-virgin olive oil.

To make the tzatziki, cut the cucumber in half and scoop out and discard the seeds. Grate it, pat the excess water off with a paper towel and stir into the yoghurt with the rest of the ingredients. Season with pepper and salt to taste.

Toss all the salad ingredients together in a bowl and serve it alongside the potatoes and the tzatziki.

BLACK BEAN TACOS
with guacamole & salsa salad

This can be quite a messy meal – which is always part of the fun. The secret to making a neat wrap is, once you've filled it, to fold over the bottom of your tortilla before you roll it. Also, I know it's hard with these delicious ingredients, but try not to over fill them as they'll only burst open when you take your first bite – I should know.

Serves 4

Ingredients for the black beans:
400g dried black/turtle beans (or 2x 400g tins)
1 tbsp vegetable oil
3 garlic cloves, chopped
3 tbsp white wine vinegar
1 1/2 tsp honey
1 1/2 tsp paprika, preferably smoked
1 1/4 tsp ground cumin

Ingredients for the salsa:
1 chilli, deseeded and finely diced
1 small red onion, finely diced
Small handful of fresh coriander, chopped
Squeeze of lime juice

Ingredients for the guacamole:
1 large avocado
Squeeze of lime
1/2 tomato, deseeded and finely diced

To serve:
8-12 tortilla, or chapatis (see page 26)
Sliced lettuce
Grated Cheddar
Tabasco sauce (optional)
Natural yoghurt
Sprinkle of paprika

Optional ingredients:
You can add other ingredients to the salsa, such as cooked sweetcorn or pomegranate seeds

If using dried beans, soak them overnight in a large bowl of cold water.

Drain the beans and place them in a medium-sized saucepan with enough fresh water to cover them and leave them, with the lid on, to simmer for about 30 minutes, or until they're soft. Drain them and set them aside.

In a large frying pan, heat the oil and the garlic gently until it's golden. Then tip in the beans, along with the vinegar, honey and spices and a pinch of salt.

Cook this on a medium heat for a further 15 minutes. If it's looking dry, add a couple of tbsp water to loosen it a little. Crush the beans gently with the back of a wooden spoon, then remove the pan from the heat.

Mix the salsa ingredients in a small bowl.

To make the guacamole, mash the avocado flesh in a bowl with the lime juice until you have a creamy texture, then mix in the diced tomato and some seasoning.

To serve, spread 1-2 heaped tablespoonfuls of beans on a warmed tortilla. Top it with a big spoonful of salsa, guacamole, a little sliced lettuce, a scattering of cheese, some Tabasco sauce and a dollop of yoghurt.

To wrap up the taco: fold the bottom end in to stop the ingredients escaping, then roll it up like a cigar.

MEDITERRANEAN SPICED PASTA
a special tomato sauce

This dish looks like a normal tomato pasta, but the Mediterranean spices lift it to another level. With all the hidden vegetables, you're going a long way towards your 5-a-day. You can store the spare spice mix in an airtight jar for another day.

Serves 4

Ingredients for the Greek spice mix:
$1/4$ tsp ground nutmeg
$1/4$ tsp coriander seeds
4 cloves
2cm cinnamon stick
$1/4$ tsp ground ginger
$1/4$ tsp chilli powder

Ingredients for the sauce:
2 tbsp olive oil
1 onion, finely diced
1 garlic clove, crushed
1 pepper, finely diced
1 carrot, finely diced
1 celery stalk, finely diced
2 x 400g tins chopped tomatoes
2 tbsp Greek spice mix

To serve:
Spaghetti
Chopped parsley if available

Make your spice mix by blending all the ingredients in a spice grinder or with a pestle and mortar.

For the sauce, heat the oil in a pan and fry the onion and garlic for 3-4 minutes. Then add the rest of the fresh vegetables and cook for around 10 more minutes.

Meanwhile, put some water and a good pinch of salt in a large pan and bring it to the boil for the spaghetti.

Pour the tinned tomatoes into the vegetable mixture with the spice mix and simmer for a further 15 minutes.

When the water has boiled, add the spaghetti and cook it according to the packet instructions, then drain it and pour it into the pasta sauce. Give it all a good stir and season to taste.

Scatter over a little chopped parsley, if you have it, before serving.

VEGGIE CHILLI
with cheesy nachos

Every family has their own chilli recipe, and this is my husband's version. If you have the time, dried beans soaked overnight work better and will be creamier in texture; they also have more time to soak up the flavour. If you have any chilli left it's great on a jacket potato the next day.

Serves 4, with leftovers

Ingredients for the chilli:
200g dried black beans (or 400g tin)
2 tbsp olive oil
I red onion, chopped
2 garlic cloves, crushed
2 x 400g tins chopped tomatoes
2 red peppers, deseeded and chopped
300ml vegetable stock
I tbsp tomato purée
400g tin kidney beans, drained

Ingredients for the sauce:
I-2 tbsp tomato purée
I tsp chilli powder
I tsp cumin seeds
2 tsp ground cumin
I tsp cayenne pepper
I tsp paprika
I tsp chilli flakes (optional)
I tsp sugar
Dash of Worcestershire sauce

Ingredients for the nachos:
200g packet tortilla chips or nachos
Handful of Cheddar
I red chilli, deseeded and finely chopped

To serve:
Natural yoghurt
Pickled chillies
Fresh coriander, chopped

Place the black beans (turtle beans) in a large bowl and soak them overnight in cold water.

Drain them, place them in a medium-szied saucepan with enough fresh water to cover them and leave them, with the lid on, to simmer for about 30 minutes, or until they're soft. Drain them and set them aside.

Heat the oil in a large saucepan and gently fry the onion and garlic together for about 10 minutes.

Add the peppers, and cook for 5 minutes, stirring all the time to stop it sticking. Add the tomatoes, purée, the black beans and half the stock. Bring it to the boil, then turn it down to a simmer.

Mix all the sauce ingredients together in the empty tomato tin with a bit more stock or hot water, then add this to the beans.

Simmer for a further 20 minutes then stir in the tinned kidney beans and any other spare beans you might have (we've used leftover baked beans and chickpeas before) and simmer for 10 more minutes.

Meanwhile, preheat the oven to 170°C and spread the tortilla chips or nachos over the bottom of an ovenproof dish. Sprinkle the cheese and chopped chilli on top and bake them until the cheese melts, about 5 minutes.

Season the chilli, and serve it with the nachos, some natural yoghurt, pickled chillies and chopped coriander.

WEEK 4

①	1 Lemon	30p	⑩	Fresh Basil 30g	70p
②	2 Limes	60p	⑪	Round/Iceberg Lettuce	40p
③	1 Large Broccoli	86p	⑫	Fresh Coriander 30g	70p
④	Carrots 1kg	45p	⑬	Cooking Peppers 600g	£1.10
⑤	1 Garlic Bulb	30p	⑭	2 Packets Salad Tomatoes 360g	£1.38
⑥	Mixed Chillies 65g	60p	⑮	Cherry Tomatoes 250g	53p
⑦	Red Onions 1kg	69p	⑯	1 Avocado	90p
⑧	White Potatoes 2.5kg	£1.29	⑰	1 Courgette	38p
⑨	1 Cucumber	50p	⑱	Mixed Sized Free Range Eggs 15 Pack	£2.00

19	British Milk 6 Pints	£1.48		**28**	Medium Noodles 300g	£1.20
20	Sour Cream 150ml	60p		**29**	Tin Chickpeas 400g	40p
21	British Mature Cheddar 450g	£2.50		**30**	Value Strawberry Jam 454g	29p
22	2 Packets British Chicken Thighs 1kg each	£5.00		**31**	Value Crunchy Peanut Butter 340g	65p
23	Value Sliced Wholemeal Bread 800g	40p		**32**	Olive Oil Spread 500g	£1.00
24	3 Packets of 8 Tortilla Wraps	£2.70		**33**	Frozen Value White Fish Fillets 520g	£1.90
25	2 Tins Value Tuna Chunks in Brine 160g	£1.30		**34**	Brown/White Onions 485g	65p
26	Value Oats 1kg	75p			Total	£35.47
27	Couscous 500g	70p			3 meals for a family of 4 x 7 days = £1.24 per person per day	

MENU FOR WEEK 4
day-by-day lower carb

Week 4 is designed as a lower carbohydrate week – not an Atkins or low carb – just a little lower than your usual. So that means no pasta, rice and not much bread; instead I've added couscous which is lower in carbs and a few potatoes or wraps.

 If you're eating less carbohydrates you'll need to add more protein to help you feel full for longer, so I've included more chicken, fish and eggs as well as other dairy products. I have again added some peanut butter as nuts are a great source of cheap protein.

 Also, instead of toast and jam for breakfast, try having porridge or an omelette.

Day 1
Lunch
Cheese quesadilla

Dinner
Chicken Fajitas with charred vegetables

Day 2
Lunch
Hummus and sliced vegetables

Dinner
Chicken in Tomatoes with onions, garlic and basil

Day 3
Lunch
Cheese wraps

Dinner
Zesty Poached Fish with roasted vegetables and couscous

Day 4
Lunch
Egg sandwiches

Dinner
Tuna Fishcakes with salad

Day 5
Lunch
Leftover couscous or cheese sandwiches

Dinner
Noodle Salad with peanut sauce

Day 6
Lunch
Cheese and tuna flaked quesadilla or leftover noodle salad

Dinner
Teriyaki-style Chicken with couscous salad

Day 7
Lunch
Chicken salad wraps

Dinner
Spanish Omelette with salad

Treat ideas
Easy Vanilla Biscuits
Flapjack
Peanut and Banana Milkshake

CHICKEN FAJITAS
with charred vegetables

We love making chicken fajitas even when we're not eating on a budget. It is a really sociable way to eat, sitting around the table together making up wraps. You can adjust the amount of chilli to make this mild or spicy hot, depending on your family's tastes.

Serves 4

Ingredients for the chicken fajitas:
4-5 chicken thighs, meat cut off the bone
3 tsp ground cumin
I tsp chilli powder
I tsp paprika
3 garlic cloves, crushed
Squeeze of lime
Dash of Tabasco
I tbsp oil, plus extra for frying
$\frac{1}{2}$ fresh chilli, finely chopped

Ingredients for the guacamole:
I large avocado, mashed
Squeeze of lime
$\frac{1}{2}$ chilli, finely chopped

Ingredients for the charred vegetables:
2 red onions, sliced into wedges
2-3 mixed colour peppers, cut into chunks

Ingredients for the salsa:
2 large tomatoes, finely chopped
$\frac{1}{2}$ red onion, finely chopped
Squeeze of lime
I tbsp white wine vinegar
I tbsp coriander, chopped

To serve:
8 tortilla wraps
100g Cheddar, grated
Splash of Tabasco
Sour cream

Mix all the fajita ingredients together in a bowl, add the chicken and make sure it gets a good coating. Cover the bowl with clingfilm and leave it for an hour or more in the fridge.

When you are ready, heat some oil in a pan and gently fry the chicken skin side down for 10-15 minutes, then turn it over to brown the other side for 3-5 minutes. Check that the juices run clear. Slice it up and put it in a bowl.

Place a griddle pan over a medium heat and char the onions and peppers for 10-15 minutes, turning them from time to time. When they're ready put them in another bowl.

To make the guacamole, mash the avocado flesh in a bowl with the lime and chilli and some seasoning until you have a creamy texture.

For the salsa, mix all the ingredients together in a bowl and season with salt to taste.

Warm the tortilla wraps as per the packet instructions and put them out on the table, along with the bowls containing the chicken, guacamole, salsa and charred vegetables.

To make up the fajitas, spoon a line of guacamole onto a tortilla, followed by a line of charred vegetables, some chicken, salsa and a scattering of grated cheese. Finish off with some dollops of sour cream and a squeeze of lime. You can add Tabasco too if you like it hot.

Fold one end in to stop the ingredients escaping, then roll the tortilla into a cigar shape and enjoy.

CHICKEN IN TOMATOES
with onions, garlic & basil

This is one of the first meals I made when I was learning to cook. It's so simple you really can't go wrong. Depending on the size of the potatoes, you can start them in the microwave to get them going, but should always finish them in the oven to make the skins nice and crispy. You could add a little cheese to the potatoes too.

Serves 4

Ingredients:
2 tbsp olive oil
1 large white onion, finely sliced
4 large chicken thighs
4 salad tomatoes, quartered
Handful of cherry tomatoes
1 pepper, deseeded and roughly chopped
$1/2$ red chilli, thinly sliced
4-6 garlic cloves, crushed
Small bunch of basil

To serve:
4 medium jacket potatoes
Knob of butter
Head of broccoli, broken into florets

Optional ingredients:
Olives, added halfway through
Bacon or chorizo, fried with the onions

Preheat the oven to 180°C.

Prick your potatoes with a fork a few times and pop them in the oven to bake for 40-60 minutes, depending on the size.

Pour half the oil in a deep-sided pan and fry the sliced onion on a low heat for about 10 minutes to soften it.

Remove the pan from the heat and add the chicken, tomatoes, pepper, chilli and garlic.

Pick half the leaves from the basil and reserve them for later. Chop up the rest with the stalks and add them to the pan with some salt and pepper and the remaining oil. Mix well and pour the mixture into an ovenproof dish and place it with the lid on in the oven for 20 minutes.

Turn the chicken pieces over and return the dish to the oven, uncovered, for another 20 minutes, or until the chicken is cooked and the skin is crispy.

The jacket potatoes should also be ready now, so carefully cut them open and add a knob of butter and some salt and pepper.

Roughly tear the remaining basil leaves and scatter them oover the chicken. Check the seasoning and serve it with the jacket potatoes and some boiled or steamed broccoli.

ZESTY POACHED FISH
with roasted peppers & couscous

Poaching is a great way of cooking fish – a healthy and delicious alternative to fried, which keeps it moist and light. Any sustainable white fish will work well. The key to poaching is to cook it very gently. The roasted peppers add colour and a sweetness to this dish, complementing the subtle flavours of the couscous and fish.

Serves 4

Ingredients:
Handful of cherry tomatoes
1½ red peppers, deseeded (1 to be saved for later in the week)
½ yellow pepper, deseeded
½ green pepper, deseeded
4 pieces of white fish
200ml milk
Knob of butter
Zest of 1½ limes or lemons, then cut into slices
1 garlic clove, sliced
1-2 bay leaves
200g couscous
300ml boiling water
¼ bunch of coriander, roughly chopped

Preheat the oven to 180°C.

Pierce the cherry tomatoes and put them with the peppers on a baking tray. Sprinkle a little oil and some salt and pepper over them. Pop them in the oven for about 20 minutes. When they've cooked slightly, dice the peppers (set aside 1 whole pepper for a recipe later in the week) and quarter the tomatoes.

Place the fish fillets in a deep frying pan and cover them with milk. Put a small knob of butter a slice of lime on each one, scatter over the garlic, half the zest, the bay leaves and some salt and pepper.

Let it simmer gently with the lid on for about 5 minutes.

Next tip your couscous into a bowl and pour the 300ml boiling water over it. Put a plate on top to keep the steam in to cook it.

After about 10 minutes the couscous should be ready and all the water absorbed. Give it a good stir with a fork to break it up then mix in the rest of the lime zest and half the chopped coriander. Put the lid back on until you are ready to serve.

Divide the couscous between 4 plates and lay the drained fish on top. Spoon a little of the poached flavoured milk over the fish with a drizzle of oil.

Before serving, scatter over the diced roasted tomatoes and peppers with the remaining coriander and a squeeze of lime.

TUNA FISHCAKES
with a mixed salad

This recipe is a great way of using up leftover breadcrumbs. For some reason my family don't like the crusts on their sandwiches, so I store them in the freezer for just this kind of dish. You can use any kind of fish, tinned, frozen or fresh; whatever is cheapest and on offer.

Serves 4

Ingredients for the fishcakes:
500g potatoes
Knob of butter, plus extra for frying
Splash of milk
1 1/2 tins (240g) tuna, drained
Zest and juice of 1/2 lemon
Handful of chopped parsley
3 tsp tomato ketchup (optional)
1 tsp Dijon mustard
1 tsp Worcestershire sauce
3 tbsp flour
1 egg, beaten
2 -3 crusts of bread for 100g breadcrumbs

Ingredients for the salad:
1/4 cucumber, sliced into chunks
2 tomatoes, diced
1/4 red onion, thinly sliced
1/4 iceberg lettuce, sliced
1/2 red or yellow pepper, deseeded and thinly sliced

To serve:
Lemon wedges
Salad

Optional ingredients:
Try using lime, grated ginger and spring onions instead of lemon and parsley in the fishcakes

Peel and chop the potatoes into small chunks. Boil them for 12-15 minutes until soft, then mash them in a bowl with a knob of butter and a splash of milk.

Mix in the tuna, the lemon zest and juice and the chopped parsley, breaking the fish apart with a fork.

Next, stir in the ketchup, mustard, Worcestershire sauce and some salt and pepper.

Divide the mixture into 4 and carefully squeeze it into balls, then squash them to make patties.

Preheat the oven to 180°C.

Put the flour, the beaten egg with some seasoning, and the breadcrumbs into 3 separate bowls.

Carefully dip the fishcakes first in the flour, then in the egg, and finally in the breadcrumbs. If they are a bit uneven don't worry; they'll look more home-made.

Chill them in the fridge for about 10 minutes, while you make up the salad.

Put a little butter in a large frying pan and gently fry the fishcakes for 2 minutes on each side until they're golden.

Transfer them to a baking tray and bake them in the oven for another 10-15 minutes.

Serve them with the salad and some lemon wedges.

NOODLE SALAD
with peanut sauce

This salad is really fresh and colourful, and with the added noodles surprisingly filling. The peanut dressing has an oriental flavour and would also work well as a dip with the Teriyaki chicken (see page 122). Please be careful if you're using a mandolin to slice your veg. I had to take my husband down to A&E the first time he used ours. I still get nervous when I see him using it.

Serves 4

Ingredients for the salad:
3-4 nests of noodles
1-2 large carrots, thinly sliced
1 courgette, thinly sliced
1 roasted pepper, cut into thin strips
$\frac{1}{2}$ red onion, thinly sliced
$\frac{1}{2}$ iceberg lettuce, sliced
1 red chilli, deseeded and sliced thinly

Ingredients for the dressing:
3 tbsp peanut butter, smooth or crunchy
2cm root ginger, grated
2 tbsp wine vinegar
$\frac{1}{2}$ tsp olive or sesame oil
2 tbsp soy sauce
1 tbsp honey
Juice of $\frac{1}{2}$ lime

To serve:
A little chopped coriander and/or mint

Optional ingredients:
Try using beetroot or mushrooms in the salad, and cashew nut butter, instead of peanut

The first thing to do is cook your noodles according to the packet instructions, as you want to add them to the salad cooled. Rinse the cooked noodles in cold water to stop them from cooking further once they are done.

Next, make the peanut dressing. Soften the peanut butter in the microwave or by heating it gently in a bowl over a saucepan of boiled water. Then mix in the rest of the dressing ingredients. You can add extra soy, honey or lime to get the flavour you want, it's just a matter of tasting it.

Mix the noodles with all the sliced salad ingredients in a large bowl and drizzle over the peanut dressing with an extra squeeze of lime, some seasoning and the chopped herbs.

TERIYAKI-STYLE CHICKEN
with couscous salad

I know how people love fried chicken shops as I see them on most high streets, but this version is much healthier as it's not deep-fried in breadcrumbs or batter. Using the cheaper cuts of meat, like the wings and thighs, is a great way to save money, too. I often cut the wings off a whole chicken when I'm jointing it and freeze them until I have enough for this dish.

Serves 4

Ingredients for the chicken:
4 chicken thighs plus any wings saved in the freezer, defrosted
2 tsp Chinese 5 spice
10cm root ginger, finely grated
2 tbsp tomato ketchup
1 garlic clove, crushed
1 tbsp soy sauce
1 tbsp honey

Ingredients for the couscous:
200g couscous
300ml boiling water
$1/4$ cucumber, deseeded and finely diced
1 large tomato, deseeded and finely diced
$1/2$ coloured pepper, deseeded and finely diced
$1/2$ small red onion, finely diced

To serve:
Sweet chilli sauce

Optional ingredients:
Tabasco if you like it spicy hot

Preheat the oven to 180°C.

Snip the corner skin of the wings and pull them open, then lay them with the chicken thighs in a snug-fitting roasting tin. Scatter over the 5 spice and some salt and pepper. Cover the tin with foil and bake them for about 40 minutes.

Mix the grated ginger in a small bowl with the ketchup, garlic, soy sauce and honey to make a glaze.

Remove the chicken from the oven and drain off any liquid in the bottom of the pan. Coat the chicken with the glaze. Return it to the oven without the foil for a further 30 minutes, or until it's golden, turning and brushing with more glaze every 10 minutes.

When the chicken is nearly cooked, make up the couscous salad by tipping the couscous into a bowl and pouring over the boiling water. Put a plate on top to keep the steam in. After about 10 minutes the couscous should be ready and all the water absorbed.

Give the couscous a good stir with a fork to break it up then stir in the diced vegetables. Put the lid back on until you are ready to serve.

Keep back a bit of cooked thigh meat to chop up and mix with mayonnaise for lunchtime wraps.

SPANISH OMELETTE
with salad

This dish is a bit like a Spanish tortilla, but with a healthy boost of colourful mixed peppers. The eggs are a great source of protein, which is especially useful if you're trying to cut back on your carbs, as it'll keep you feeling fuller for longer.

Serves 4

Ingredients for the omelette:
2 tbsp oil
4 medium potatoes, diced small
$^3/_4$ red onion, finely sliced
3 garlic cloves, squashed but left whole
$^1/_4$ each of 4 mixed coloured peppers, deseeded and diced
$^1/_2$ tsp paprika
$^1/_2$ tsp dried oregano or thyme
6 eggs

Ingredients for the salad:
$^1/_4$ cucumber, diced
2 tomatoes, diced
$^1/_4$ red onion, thinly sliced
$^1/_4$ iceberg lettuce, sliced
$^1/_2$ red or yellow pepper, cut into batons
1 carrot, cut into batons

Put the oil in a large ovenproof frying pan and sauté the sliced onions, potatoes and garlic for about 10 minutes on a medium heat.

Add the diced peppers, sprinkle over the paprika and herbs and continue frying for another 10 minutes, until the potatoes are soft and the peppers cooked.

Whisk the eggs in a bowl with a little salt and pepper and add them to the frying pan. Turn the heat up for a few minutes while you stir gently.

Once the eggs start to set around the sides, put the pan under the grill for 4-5 minutes, or until the top is set, golden and fluffy.

Cut it into slices and serve warm or cold with the salad.

WEEK 5

1	2 Limes		60p	**11**	Celery		55p
2	Ripe Bananas 5 Pack		80p	**12**	1 Cucumber		50p
3	1 Large Broccoli		86p	**13**	Fresh Coriander 30g		70p
4	Carrots 1kg		45p	**14**	Mixed Chillies 65g		60p
5	2 Garlic Bulbs		60p	**15**	Round Lettuce		40p
6	2 Aubergines		£1.40	**16**	Cooking Peppers 600g		£1.10
7	Red Onions 1kg		69p	**17**	Bunch of Spring Onions 100g		49p
8	White Potatoes 2.5kg		£1.29	**18**	Packet Salad Tomatoes 360g		69p
9	Butternut Squash		90p	**19**	Olive Oil Spread 500g		£1.00
10	4 Avocados		£1.75	**20**	Mixed Sized Free Range Eggs 15 Pack		£2.00

21	British Milk 6 Pints		£1.48	**31**	Tomato Purée Tube 200g	40p
22	British Mature Cheddar 350g		£2.00	**32**	Couscous 500g	70p
23	Medium Sliced Wholemeal Bread 800g		40p	**33**	Value Strawberry Jam 454g	29p
24	2 packets of 8 Tortilla Wraps		£1.80	**34**	Value Crunchy Peanut Butter 340g	65p
25	Value Lightly Salted Tortillas 200g		46p	**35**	Value Garden Peas 900g	69p
26	Value Oats 1kg		75p		Total	£33.20
27	Tin Chickpeas 400g		50p			
28	Black Turtle Beans 500g		£1.80			
29	Frozen Soya Mince 454g		£1.75			
30	6 Tins Value Chopped Tomatoes 400g		£1.86		3 meals for a family of 4 × 7 days = £1.18 per person per day	

MENU FOR WEEK 5
day-by-day lower-carb vegetarian

Week 5 is designed as a lower-carbohydrate vegetarian week so again no refined white pasta, bread or rice; instead I've added butternut squash and soya mince, which is a great source of protein.

If you're cutting back on carbohydrates and avoiding meats you'll have to think really carefully about how to get more protein to maintain a balanced diet – more beans and pulses, as well as the trusty eggs, would be good.

The shopping list includes plenty of vegetables and salad to help towards your 5-a-day.

Day 1
Lunch
Pea and mint soup

Dinner
Black Beans with tortilla and omelette

Day 2
Lunch
Cheese and avocado quesadilla

Dinner
Butternut Tagine with lime & coriander couscous

Day 3
Lunch
Black bean soup or cheese sandwiches

Dinner
Moussaka with a simple salad

Day 4
Lunch
Leftover tagine or cheese sandwiches

Dinner
Spanish Tortilla with rosemary & salad

Day 5
Lunch
Leftover Moussaka or cheese salad wraps

Dinner
Huevos Rancheros

Day 6
Lunch
Cheese salad sandwiches

Dinner
Soya Mince Hotpot with broccoli

Day 7
Lunch
Leftover Hotpot or cheese sandwiches

Dinner
Enchiladas

Snack ideas
Flapjack
Banana Bread
Cheesy nachos
Peanut and Banana Milkshake

BLACK BEANS
with tortillas & omelette

This meal is inspired by a dish from Costa Rica called *gallo pinto*, and would traditionally be cooked with rice. There isn't any on the current shopping list as it's a low-carb week, but feel free to add some when you make it another time.

Serves 4

Ingredients for the black beans:
150g dried black beans, soaked overnight
2 tbsp vegetable oil, 1 for frying eggs
1 red onion, chopped
2 garlic cloves, chopped
1 tsp ground cumin
1 tsp ground coriander
4 tbsp Worcestershire sauce
1/4 tsp chilli flakes or cayenne pepper

Ingredients for the dressing:
1 garlic clove, finely chopped
Handful of fresh coriander, chopped
2 spring onions, chopped
Zest and juice of 1 lime
1 tbsp vegetable oil
1 tsp caster sugar

To serve:
4-egg omelette
Chapattis / tortilla (see page 26)
Lime wedges
Tomatoes, sliced
2 avocados, sliced
Sprinkle of fresh coriander (optional)

Drain the beans, place them in a medium-sized saucepan with enough fresh water to cover them. Simmer them, with the lid on for about 30 minutes, or until they're soft. Drain them and set them aside.

This would be a good time to make your tortillas (see page 26).

Next, pour the oil into a large frying pan on a medium heat. Add the onion and cook it for 10 minutes. Stir in the garlic, cumin and coriander and cook for 1 more minute. Then mix in the cooked beans with the Worcestershire sauce and chilli and cook for about 3 minutes more, stirring occasionally. Add a splash of water if it starts to go dry. Season to taste with salt and pepper.

Mix all the dressing ingredients together in a small bowl and season to taste.

To make the omelette, crack the eggs into a bowl with a knob of butter and some seasoning and beat well with a fork.

Heat the oil in a frying pan and add the beaten eggs. As it cooks, push the set parts into the centre. When the underside is done, flip it over and cook the other side.

Serve the black beans and omelette with a tortilla, a wedge of lime, some sliced tomatoes and avocados drizzled with the zesty dressing and a sprinkle of coriander.

BUTTERNUT TAGINE
with lime & coriander couscous

You don't have to use a tagine to cook this – the recipe works just as well with a large saucepan. This is another dish that tastes better the next day so you could make it in advance and reheat it. You can also save some of the couscous for lunches; I like adding hummus or sweet chilli to mine.

Serves 4

Ingredients for the tagine:
2 tbsp oil
1-2 red onions, chopped into thin wedges
4 garlic cloves, chopped
$^1/_2$ cinnamon stick or 1 tsp ground cinnamon
1 tsp coriander seeds
$^1/_2$ tsp ground ginger
2 tsp cumin seeds
$^1/_2$ bunch of coriander, stalks chopped (save the leaves for garnishing)
400g tin chopped tomatoes
1 butternut squash, peeled and diced
2 medium-sized carrots, diced
850ml vegetable stock
400g tin chickpeas
$^1/_2$ tsp chilli flakes
3 tbsp sultanas (optional)

Ingredients for the couscous:
200g couscous
300ml boiling water
Zest and juice of 1 lime
$^1/_2$ bunch of coriander, chopped

Optional ingredients:
You can add apricots instead of sultanas and flaked, toasted almonds before serving

Heat the oil in a large saucepan pan or tagine and fry the onions and garlic for a few minutes. Then add the spices and half the chopped coriander stalks and cook for a minute or so until it begins to smell aromatic.

Add the tinned tomatoes, butternut squash, carrots and vegetable stock and give it all a good stir, making sure the liquid covers the vegetables. Bring it to the boil, then put the lid on and turn it down to a very gentle simmer for about 30 minutes, stirring occasionally.

Next, add the chickpeas, chilli flakes and sultanas. Let it simmer for another 15-20 minutes, or until the butternut squash and carrots are soft but not mushy, and the sauce has thickened.

When the cooking time is nearly up, tip the couscous into a bowl and pour boiling water over it. Put a plate on top to retain the steam to cook the couscous. After 8-10 minutes the couscous should be ready and all the water absorbed.

Give the couscous a good stir with a fork to break it up then mix in the lime zest and juice and chopped coriander.

Serve the tagine with the couscous and scatter over the saved coriander leaves to garnish.

MOUSSAKA
with a simple salad

Moussaka may seem quite complicated to make, but really it's just like a lasagna in its construction. This version uses black beans instead of mince. If you can, add a glass of red wine to the tomato sauce for more depth of flavour.

Serves 4

Ingredients for the moussaka:
150g dried black beans, soaked overnight
1 red onion, finely chopped
2 garlic cloves, crushed
1 tsp dried oregano
1 tsp dried mint
2 bay leaves
$1/2$ tsp ground cinnamon
5 tbsp olive oil
400g tin chopped tomatoes
2 tbsp tomato purée
2 aubergines, cut into 1cm slices
500g potatoes, peeled and sliced into 1cm discs
600ml white sauce (see page 45)
$1/4$ tsp grated nutmeg
1 egg, beaten
25g cheese, finely grated

Ingredients for the salad:
$1/4$ iceberg lettuce
$1/4$ cucumber, diced
2 large tomatoes, diced
2 celery stalks, finely sliced

Drain the black beans and place them in a medium-sized saucepan with enough fresh water to cover them. Leave them, with the lid on, to simmer for about 30 minutes, or until they're soft. Drain them and set them aside.

Preheat the oven to 180°C.

In a saucepan over a medium heat, cook the onions, garlic, oregano, mint, bay leaves and cinnamon in 2 tbsp oil for 10 minutes. Then add the tomatoes, tomato purée, black beans and a splash of water and bring it to a simmer. Leave it for another 10 minutes, stirring occasionally, until the sauce has thickened. Season with salt and pepper.

Heat 3 tbsp oil in a frying pan and cook the aubergines for 2-3 minutes on each side, then place them on kitchen paper to soak up the excess oil. Alternatively, if you want to use less oil, cook them on a griddle pan.

Meanwhile parboil the potatoes in salted water for 5 minutes, then drain them in a colander.

For the white sauce follow the method on page 45. After you have made it, quickly stir in the grated nutmeg, some seasoning and the beaten egg.

To assemble the moussaka, spoon half the bean sauce into a large, shallow ovenproof dish. Cover this with a layer of potatoes, then a layer of aubergines. Repeat the layers, finishing with aubergines. Pour the white sauce over the top, making sure it spreads in a thick, even layer.

Sprinkle the cheese and grind some black pepper over the top, and bake it in the oven for 45 minutes, or until the surface is golden brown and bubbling.

SPANISH-STYLE TORTILLA
with rosemary & salad

Tortilla is a delicious tapas dish that you'll see in every bar in Spain. This version is a twist on the original, using an aromatic combination of red onions and rosemary with the potatoes. It's a real crowd pleaser, and what's more, it's just as good cold so if there's any left over you can have it for lunch the next day.

Serves 4

Ingredients for the tortilla:
2 tbsp oil
I red onion, finely diced
300g potatoes, finely diced
I sprig of rosemary, leaves only, finely chopped
6 eggs
I tsp mixed herbs

Ingredients for the salad:
2 large tomatoes, cut into chunks
$^1/_4$ iceberg lettuce
$^1/_4$ cucumber
2 celery stalks, finely sliced

Optional ingredients:
You could use sweet potatoes, and maybe add I tsp of wholegrain mustard to the egg mixture

Heat the oil in a large non-stick, ovenproof frying pan and gently sauté the onions, potatoes and rosemary with a pinch of salt, stirring frequently for about 25 minutes or until the potatoes are soft.

Whisk the eggs in a bowl with the herbs and some seasoning then pour them into the frying pan. Cook the tortilla gently for about 10 minutes on a low heat.

Once it starts to set around the sides, put it under the grill for 4-5 minutes, or until the top is golden and set. Scatter over a few more rosemary leaves.

Cut the tortilla into slices and serve it warm or cold with a salad.

HUEVOS RANCHEROS
spicy eggs with tortillas

I'm using this dish as an evening meal for this budget week, but in fact huevos rancheros is a traditional Mexican breakfast. You can make it as hot and spicy as you like by adding Tabasco sauce at the end.

Serves 4

Ingredients:
2 tbsp olive oil
3 red onions, finely chopped
2 green peppers, finely chopped
2 red peppers, finely chopped
4 garlic cloves, finely chopped
2 red chillies, finely chopped
3-4 fresh bay leaves
2 tbsp tomato pureé
2 × 400g tins chopped tomato
2 tsp sugar
25g butter
4 eggs

To serve:
Handful of coriander leaves, chopped
Tabasco sauce
8 chapatis/ tortillas (see page 26)
Handful of grated Cheddar
Chilli sauce

Firstly, make your tortillas, and keep them warm in foil in a low oven.

To make the sauce, pour the oil into a large lidded frying pan over a low to medium heat and fry the onions, peppers, garlic, chillies and bay leaves, for about 15 minutes, stirring occasionally.

Then add the tomato pureé and tinned tomatoes and allow the sauce to simmer for a further 10 minutes with the lid off, stirring occasionally. Season it with sugar, salt and pepper.

Take out half of the salsa to use for a meal later in the week, let it cool, then pop it into the fridge.

Make 4 depressions in the remaining salsa, and place a small knob of butter in the middle of each one.

Break an egg into each hole, and put the lid on the pan and poach the eggs for roughly 2 minutes. They are ready when the whites are firm and opaque.

To finish, sprinkle the dish with chopped coriander leaves and a splash of Tabasco and serve it with the warm tortillas, grated cheese and chilli sauce.

SOYA MINCE HOTPOT
with broccoli

This is a hearty, warming meal, and if you're trying to cut back on the carbs, the topping of thinly sliced potato instead of heavy mash is an easy way to achieve that. Soya mince is also a healthy option as it has less saturated fat than meat.

Serves 4 (with leftovers)

Ingredients:
25g butter
1 red onion, chopped
2 carrots, diced
2 garlic cloves, finely chopped
250g soya mince
1 tbsp dried thyme
2 bay leaves
50ml red wine (optional)
Dash of Worcestershire sauce
1 tbsp tomato purée
400ml vegetable stock
100g frozen peas, defrosted
3 medium potatoes
Drizzle of olive oil
50g Cheddar, grated

To serve:
Broccoli

To make the mince, melt the butter in a large pan, then gently fry the onion, carrots and garlic for 15 minutes with the lid on until they're soft and lightly golden.

Stir in the soya mince and herbs, followed by the wine, Worcestershire sauce, tomato purée and stock. Bring it to the boil, turn it down to a simmer, with the lid off, for 30-40 minutes or until the liquid starts to thicken. Then stir in the peas.

Preheat the oven to 190°C.

While the sauce is cooking, cut the potatoes into 5mm slices and simmer them in a pan of salted boiling water for a couple of minutes so they are partly cooked but haven't lost their shape. Drain them well.

To assemble the hotpot, pour the sauce into a deep casserole dish and cover it with one or two layers of potato, drizzled with oil, and a sprinkle of salt and pepper. Scatter the cheese on top and bake it for 30 minutes or until the topping is golden.

Serve it with boiled or steamed broccoli.

ENCHILADAS

The first time I cooked this dish it was because I wanted to use up some leftover chilli con carne at the back of the fridge, and it was such a success I now make it regularly. These enchiladas are made with the leftover salsa from the Huevos Rancheros mixed with the last of the soya mince – a neat way to end the week.

Serves 4

Ingredients:
The leftover cooked salsa from the rancheros
200g soya mince (rest of the packet)
1 tbsp oil
8 tortilla wraps
75g Cheddar

To serve:
Pickled chillies
Handful of fresh coriander, chopped
Salad

Optional ingredients:
You can make enchiladas with different fillings, for example, black beans or kidney beans, or for meat eaters: chicken and cheese or minced beef

Preheat the oven to 200°C.

Tip the leftover salsa and the soya mince into a large pan and mix them together well. Heat the mixture on a low setting, stirring occasionally.

Brush the inside of a large ovenproof serving dish with a little oil. Lay one of the tortillas in the dish and spoon $\frac{1}{8}$ the salsa mixture into the centre.

Roll the tortilla and push it to the side. Repeat until all the tortillas and salsa mixture are used. You should have 8 filled, rolled tortillas resting tightly side by side.

Grate over the cheese and bake the enchiladas for about 20 minutes or until the cheese is golden brown and bubbling.

Add a splash of Tabasco if you like them hot, and a scattering of coriander and pickled chillies and serve them with a salad.

WEEK 6

1	Closed Cup Mushrooms 300g	86p		**11**	White Potatoes 2.5kg	£1.29
2	3 Limes	90p		**12**	Bunch of Bananas	80p
3	1 Broccoli	86p		**13**	Celery	55p
4	Carrots 1kg	45p		**14**	1 Cucumber	50p
5	2 Garlic Bulbs	30p		**15**	2 Bunches of Fresh Coriander	£1.40
6	Mixed Chillies 65g	60p		**16**	Round/Iceberg Lettuce	40p
7	Cooking Peppers 600g	£1.10		**17**	Lemongrass 2 stalks	70p
8	Red Onions 1kg	69p		**18**	Packet Salad Tomatoes	69p
9	Root Ginger 100g	26p		**19**	Violife Vegan Cheese	£2.30
10	Trimmed Salad Onions	49p		**20**	4 UHT Unsweetened Soya Drink 1 Litre	£2.36

21	Vitalite Dairy Free Spread 500g	£1.02	**31**	3 Tins Coconut Milk 400ml	£2.25
22	Value Oats 1kg	75p	**32**	2 Tins Butter Beans 400g	76p
23	4 Tins Chopped Tomatoes 400g	£1.24	**33**	2 Tins Chickpeas 400g	80p
24	Tin Sweetcorn 326g	35p	**34**	Couscous 500g	70p
25	Clarks Original Maple Syrup 180ml	£1.98	**35**	Value Strawberry Jam 454g	29p
26	2 Packets Strong Brown Flour 1.5kg each	£2.00	**36**	Value Crunchy Peanut Butter 340g	65p
27	Plain Flour 1.5kg	60p	**37**	Value Garden Peas 900g	69p
28	Alpro Simply Plain Soya Yoghurt 500g	£1.37	**38**	1 Cauliflower	£1.00
29	Frozen Whole Leaf Spinach 1kg	£1.40		Total	£37.43
30	Frozen Summer Fruit Mix 500g	£2.00		3 meals for a family of 4 x 7 days = £1.33 per person per day	

MENU FOR WEEK 6
day-by-day vegan

A vegan week was a bit of a challenge the first time I designed one for my blog. I wasn't sure what was involved in a vegan diet but have since found and adjusted loads of great recipes to fit. Specialist vegan food can be expensive so you have to be careful to keep within budget.

To maintain the protein content, I have added more soya, spinach, peanut butter and beans. The extra price for vegan cheese means I've kept it to a minimum – really just for sandwiches.

Some breakfast ideas this week include porridge with maple syrup or vegan yoghurt and berries or, if you have more time at weekends, vegan pancakes (see page 49). I have also budgeted for making your own bread as you can't guarantee shop bought is vegan without paying a lot for it.

Day 1
Lunch
Pea and mint soup

Dinner
Steamed Dim Sum with vegetables and dips

Day 2
Lunch
Hummus and crudités or bread

Dinner
Baked Butter Bean Stew & home-made bread

Day 3
Lunch
Leftover Butter Bean Stew or vegan cheese salad sandwich

Dinner
Potato & Spinach Curry with chapatis

Day 4
Lunch
Leftover curry or vegan cheese salad sandwich

Dinner
Nettle Pasta in a Spicy Sauce with garlic bread

Day 5
Lunch
Cold pasta salad

Dinner
Thai Green Curry with chapati

Day 6
Lunch
Couscous salad

Dinner
Vegan Burgers with chips and salad

Day 7
Lunch
Salad bowl

Dinner
Roasted Cauliflower & couscous

Treat ideas
Vegan Berry Muffins
Vegan Pancakes
Peanut Butter and Banana Milkshakes
Healthy Brownies

STEAMED DIM SUM
with vegetables & dips

Coconut milk is a great alternative to dairy for vegans. You can eat these delicious dim sum buns as they are, or fry them in groundnut oil after steaming, or add them to a vegetable stock soup with some frozen spinach. The bamboo baskets can be picked up quite cheaply from Asian supermarkets.

Serves 4

Ingredients for the filling:
3 garlic cloves, finely sliced
2.5cm root ginger, grated
$1/2$ bunch of fresh coriander, chopped
Groundnut oil
150g mushrooms, finely chopped
3 tbsp rice wine (or white wine) vinegar
3 tbsp sweet chilli sauce
3 tbsp soy sauce
3 spring onions, finely sliced
1 large carrot, grated
1 fresh chilli, finely sliced
1 tbsp sesame oil (or olive oil)

Ingredients for the bun:
400ml tin coconut milk
500g self-raising flour, plus extra for dusting
Pinch of sea salt
2 tbsp sesame seeds (optional)

To serve:
Hoisin sauce (optional)
Sweet chilli sauce
2-3 spring onions, cut in half and sliced lengthwise
$1/4$ cucumber, deseeded and sliced lengthwise

On a medium-high heat, sauté the garlic, ginger and coriander with the groundnut oil in a large frying pan. Add the mushrooms and fry for 5 more minutes.

Pour the vinegar, sweet chilli sauce and soy sauce into the pan and cook for a further 5 minutes, or until the mushrooms are begin to caramelise. Transfer to a bowl and stir in the spring onions, carrot, chilli and sesame oil and set aside.

To make the bun dough, blend the coconut milk and flour with a good pinch of salt in a food processor or beat them together in a bowl with a wooden spoon. Transfer the dough to a flour-dusted surface and roll it into a thick sausage. Cut it into 12 equal-sized pieces. Roll these into balls and then flatten them into rounds, roughly $1/2$ cm thick.

Now to assemble the dim sum. Divide the mushroom mixture equally between the 12 dough circles (you'll need roughly 1 tbsp filling per circle), making sure to leave a 2cm gap around the edges. Bring up the sides and fold them around the filling, pinching the edges together to enclose it.

Place the dim sum upside down (so the scruffy edges are underneath) on greaseproof paper with slits in and place them in the two bamboo steamer baskets – you'll need 2 for 12 buns.

Bring 1 litre of water to the boil in a large saucepan, pop the steamer baskets on top. Reduce the heat to medium and steam the dim sum for around 12 minutes, or until they're piping hot and puffed up.

Once the buns are ready, sprinkle over the seeds, and serve them with some sauce and the sliced spring onions and cucumber.

BAKED BUTTER BEAN STEW

I used foraged nettles in the original recipe for this dish on my blog, but if you're not brave enough to do that, frozen spinach is fine. The tomatoes really compliment the creamy texture of the butter beans. Although I used tinned beans, dried ones soaked overnight would work just as well.

Serves 4

Ingredients:
2 onions, chopped
2 garlic cloves, chopped
6 tbsp olive oil
1 tbsp sweet paprika
1 tbsp tomato purée
2 x 400g tins chopped tomatoes
3 large handfuls of frozen spinach
2 x 400g tins butter beans
Small handful of fresh parsley, chopped
Small handful of fresh mint, chopped
1 tsp dried oregano

To serve:
Home-made bread (see page 20)

Preheat the oven to 160°C.

Place a large saucepan over a medium heat and gently fry the onions and garlic in 2 tbsp of the olive oil for 5 minutes.

Stir in the paprika, tomato purée, chopped tomatoes, 100ml water and some seasoning.

Bring the pan to the boil then reduce the heat and let it simmer for 30 minutes.

Add the spinach and butter beans to the stew. After a couple of minutes remove it from the heat and add the chopped herbs.

Transfer the stew to a casserole, drizzle over the remaining olive oil and bake it for 25-30 minutes or until the sauce has thickened.

Serve it with fresh bread – you'll want to mop up the juices.

Save some if you can as it tastes even better the next day.

POTATO & SPINACH CURRY
with home-made chapatis

This dish is a regular family favourite even though we're not vegan. I always have a bag of spinach in the freezer so I can make this whenever we have a craving for it. The curry paste will last for at least a week in the fridge, so you can make it at the weekend to be used midweek. For variation, try using new potatoes, if in season, or butternut squash.

Serves 4

Ingredients for the curry paste:
3 tsp cumin seeds
2 tsp coriander seeds
1 tsp black peppercorns
2 garlic cloves
2.5cm root ginger, peeled
100g fresh coriander
2 onions
1 tsp paprika
2 tsp garam masala
1 tsp ground turmeric
$1/2$ tsp salt
2 tbsp oil
1 tbsp tomato purée
$1/2$ tsp chilli seeds

Ingredients for the curry:
1 tbsp olive oil
4 large potatoes, skins left on, diced
2 tomatoes, finely diced
2 tbsp curry paste (see below)
1-2 peppers, deseeded and roughly chopped
200g frozen spinach, defrosted
3 tbsp vegan yogurt

To serve:
Home-made chapatis (see page 26)
Chilli, deseeded and finely chopped
Handful of fresh coriander, chopped
Vegan yoghurt

Start by making the curry paste. Toast the cumin and coriander seeds with the peppercorns in a dry pan shaking them until they start to release their smell. Crush them to a powder with a pestle and mortar.

Then put them with all the other curry paste ingredients, in a blender and blitz to form a thick paste. Set it aside for later.

Heat the oil in a large saucepan and gently fry the potatoes for 3-4 minutes. Then add the tomatoes and curry paste with a pinch of salt and pepper and fry for 5 more minutes.

Pour in enough boiling water to half cover the potatoes, stir and cover it with a lid. Bring it to the boil then turn the heat down and let it simmer for about 10 minutes or until the potaotes are cooked through but still quite firm.

(You can make the chapati dough while this is simmering so they are ready to cook when the curry is ready.)

Remove the lid, then add the peppers and let it bubble away for about 10-15 minutes, or until the liquid is reduced. Stir occasionally to stop it sticking.

When the potatoes and peppers are nearly ready, squeeze the liquid out of the spinach and add it to the curry. Let it simmer for a further 5 minutes, while you cook the chapatis.

Serve the curry with chopped coriander scattered on top and vegan yoghurt and chapatis on the side.

NETTLE PASTA IN A SPICY SAUCE
with garlic bread

OK, so you don't have to make this with nettles; you could use spinach instead (see recipe on page 19). By making your own fresh pasta you know it won't contain a trace of egg, and you can make as much or as little as you want by adjusting the ingredients so there isn't any waste either.

Serves 4

Ingredients for the pasta:
200g nettles
400g fresh vegan pasta (see page 16)

Ingredients for the sauce:
1 tbsp oil
1 red onion, sliced
1 chilli pepper, thinly sliced
2 garlic cloves, thinly sliced
1 x 400g tin chopped tomatoes

Optional ingredients:
Glass of red wine
Black pitted olives, chopped
1 tbsp capers

To serve:
Fresh parsley

Ingredients for the garlic bread:
4 slices of home-made vegan bread (see page 22)
1 garlic clove, sliced in half
Drizzle of olive oil
Salt

Wash the nettles and boil them for a few minutes to take out the sting. Whizz them in a blender to make a paste. You can use spinach if you prefer.

Next, make the sauce. Heat the oil in a saucepan and fry the onion for 10 minutes then add the garlic and chilli and cook for a further 5 minutes. Pour in the tomatoes and simmer for 10-15 minutes more. You can add a glass of wine, some chopped olives and capers here if you want. Season it now to taste.

Roll the pasta dough out very thinly, aiming for 1-2mm in thickness. (see page 16 for tips). Then, with a sharp knife, cut it into fine tagliatelle-shaped strips.

Gently tip the pasta into a large pan of salted boiling water and cook it for 2-3 minutes. Check it's cooked to your liking before draining it in a colander.

Return the pasta to the empty pan and stir in the tomato sauce. Scatter over a little chopped parsley and a handful of vegan cheese if you have it.

For the garlic bread, toast slices of your bread on a griddle pan then rub the toast with the halves of garlic. Drizzle with extra virgin olive oil and sprinkle with a little salt.

THAI GREEN CURRY
with chapatis

This is another of our family favourites. What makes this special is the curry paste made from scratch. With no preservatives in it, it is far better for you, plus it really zings. You can experiment with different leftover vegetables – just make sure they are cut the same size so that they all take the same time to cook. This recipe includes chapatis but you could just as easily have brown rice.

Serves 4

Ingredients for the curry paste:
4 garlic cloves
I small onion
I thumb-sized piece of ginger
2 lemongrass stalks
I-2 chillies
I tsp ground cumin
½ bunch of fresh coriander

Ingredients for the curry:
150g mushrooms
I tbsp groundnut oil
2 x 400ml tins coconut milk
Vegetable stock cube
6 kaffir lime leaves (optional)
I broccoli, cut into florets
200g frozen peas
Juice of 1-2 limes

To serve:
Handful of fresh coriander, chopped
I spring onion, finely sliced
Lime wedges
Home-made chapatis (see page 26)

To make the curry paste, peel, roughly chop and place the garlic, onions and ginger in a food processor.

Trim the lemongrass, remove the tough outer leaves, then finely chop it and add it to the processor. Cut the stalks off the chillies and put them in too, along with the cumin and half the coriander, stalks and all. Blitz it until you have a smooth paste.

Cut the mushrooms in half and fry them in the oil in a large saucepan for 4 to 5 minutes Transfer them to a plate using a slotted spoon.

Reduce the heat to medium-low and fry the curry paste for 4 to 5 minutes, stirring occasionally.

Pour in the coconut milk and 200ml boiling water, crumble in the stock cube with the lime leaves. Turn the heat up and bring it the boil, then let it simmer for 10 minutes, or until it has reduced slightly.

Prepare the chapatis while the curry is cooking and keep them warm in foil in a low oven.

Stir in the mushrooms into the sauce and cook for a further 5 minutes, then add the broccoli and peas. After another 5 minutes the vegetables should be cooked but firm.

Season to taste with lime juice, salt and freshly ground black pepper. Before serving, stir through the coriander and spring onion. Serve it with lime wedges and the chapatis.

VEGAN BURGERS
with chips & salad

These vegan burgers are a long way from the bean burgers you get from fast-food outlets. With their crispy outsides and flavourful insides, they're a real treat. The burgers sit in toasted home-made rolls with all the trimmings of a traditional takeaway, including fat home-made chips.

Serves 4

Ingredients for the burgers:
400g tin chickpeas
340g tin sweetcorn
1 tsp paprika
1 tsp ground coriander
1 tsp ground cumin
Zest of 1 lemon
3 heaped tbsp flour, plus extra for dusting
Sea salt
Rapeseed oil for frying

For the garnish:
Tomato ketchup
Lettuce leaves, washed
2 large ripe tomatoes, sliced
$^1/_2$ red onion, thinly sliced (optional)

To serve
Home-made rolls (see page 20)
Potato wedges (see page 70)
Salad

Drain the chickpeas and sweetcorn and tip them into a food processor with the spices, lemon zest, flour and a pinch of salt, then pulse until everything is combined, but not too smooth – you want to keep a bit of texture.

On a flour-dusted surface, divide and shape the mixture into 4 equally sized patties (roughly 2cm thick), or 8 thinner ones if you want them crispier.

Pop them onto a tray and place them in the fridge for around 30 minutes to firm up.

Place a large frying pan over a medium heat and add a splash of oil. Once it's hot, fry the patties for 10 minutes, or until they're golden, turning them halfway through.

Toast the inside of each roll. Squeeze a large dollop of ketchup onto the base of the rolls, then place the burgers on top.

Layer over a couple of slices of tomato, a lettuce leaf, some onion, and finally the roll tops.

Serve them with potato wedges and a salad.

ROASTED CAULIFLOWER
& herby couscous

Cauliflower seems to be very popular at the moment. If it's not being made into substitute rice, it's being used as pizza bases. I prefer to eat mine baked in the oven with delicious herbs and spices.

Serves 4

Ingredients for the cauliflower:
1 large cauliflower, broken into florets
2 red peppers, thickly sliced
2 or 3 red onions, thickly sliced
3 tbsp olive oil
1 tbsp ground cumin
1 tbsp ground coriander
1 tsp chilli flakes
1 tsp fennel seeds
1 tsp ground turmeric (optional)

Ingredients for the couscous:
200g couscous
300ml boiling water
4 or 5 baby tomatoes, finely chopped
1 red onion, finely chopped
1 celery stalk, finely sliced
$1/4$ cucumber, deseeded and finely sliced

Ingredients for the dressing:
1 tbsp lemon juice
2 tbsp olive oil
1 garlic clove, crushed
Few parsley sprigs, chopped
Few mint sprigs, chopped
$1/2$ tsp chilli flakes

To serve:
Vegan yoghurt with a pinch of paprika

Preheat the oven to 200°C.

Put the cauliflower florets, peppers and red onions on a baking tray and toss them in the oil. Mix all the spices together and sprinkle them over the veg, then roast them in the oven for about 25 minutes.

While the vegetables are cooking, put the couscous in a medium-sized bowl and pour the boiling water over it. Put a plate on top to keep the steam in to cook it and leave for 10 minutes.

To make the dressing, mix all the ingredients together in a small bowl or jar and season to taste with salt and pepper.

When you are ready to eat, stir the salad ingredients into the couscous in a large serving dish. Pile the roasted vegetables on top, then pour the herby dressing over. Serve it with a small bowl of vegan yoghurt sprinkled with paprika.

WEEK 7

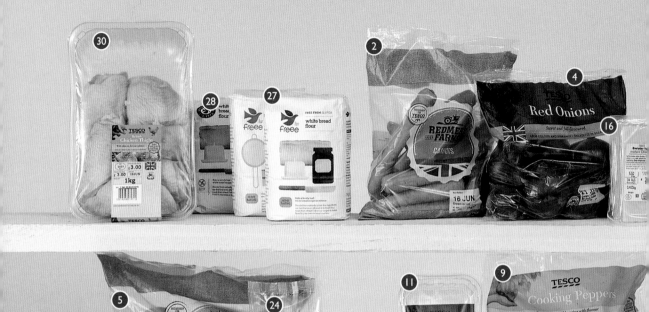

1	2 Lemons	60p	10	Packet Salad Tomatoes 360g	69p
2	Carrots 1kg	45p	11	Cherry Tomatoes 250g	53p
3	2 Garlic Bulbs	60p	12	Celery	55p
4	Red Onions 1kg	69p	13	Olive Oil Spread 500g	£1.00
5	White Potatoes 2.5kg	£1.29	14	12 Medium Free Range Eggs	£1.75
6	Fresh Basil	70p	15	British Milk 6 Pints	£1.48
7	Mixed Chillies 65g	60p	16	Cheddar Cheese 350g	£2.00
8	Round/Iceberg Lettuce	40p	17	Mozzarella Cheese 125g	47p
9	Cooking Peppers 600g	£1.10	18	Finest Spanish Chorizo 225g	£2.50

19	Newburn Bakehouse Mini Loaf Seeded 300g	£1.75	28	Doves Farm Gluten-free Bread Flour 1kg	£1.70
20	Value Oats 1kg	75p	29	Doves Farm Xanthan Gum 100g	£2.30
21	2 Tins Chickpeas 400g	£1.00	30	British Chicken Thighs 1kg	£2.50
22	3 Tins Chopped Tomatoes 400g	93p	31	Frozen Jumbo Raw King Prawns 240g	£3.00
23	Tomato Purée Tube 200g	40p	32	Value Garden Peas 900g	69p
24	Lentils 500g	£1.15	33	Root Ginger 50g	15p
25	Arborio Risotto Rice 500g	£1.10	34	Fresh Coriander 30g	70p
26	Value Strawberry Jam 454g	29p		Total	£36.71
27	2 Doves Farm Gluten-free Plain Flour 1kg	£3.40		3 meals for a family of 4 x 7 days = £1.31 per person per day

MENU FOR WEEK 7
day-by-day gluten-free

Week 6 is for anyone on a gluten-free diet, whether it's through choice or because you're a coeliac. Hopefully you'll find some recipes here that will help you save money, as gluten-free products can be very expensive.

I've added porridge for breakfast for most days as oats are gluten-free, but I have included a loaf of gluten-free bread as an alternative. It's much cheaper to make your own – see my sample recipe on page 22.

As well as risotto rice dishes I have given recipes for gluten-free pizza and curry so no one needs to miss out on treat nights.

Day 1
Lunch
Lentil soup and gluten-free bread

Dinner
Gluten-Free Chicken Curry with onion bhajis & chapatis

Day 2
Lunch
Leftover curry or cheese sandwiches on gluten-free bread

Dinner
Chicken Paella with prawns & chorizo

Day 3
Lunch
Leftover paella or egg sandwiches on gluten-free bread

Dinner
Gluten-free Pizza with a vegetarian topping

Day 4
Lunch
Hummus and crudités

Dinner
Pea & Mint Risotto with lemon zest

Day 5
Lunch
Egg sandwiches on gluten-free bread

Dinner
Patatas Bravas with salad

Day 6
Lunch
Pea soup and gluten-free bread

Dinner
Spicy Chorizo Pasta with garlic bread

Day 7
Lunch
Cold pasta salad

Dinner
Arancini with salad and aioli

Treat ideas
Gluten-free Anzac Biscuits
Flapjack
Pavlova with Fruit

GLUTEN-FREE CHICKEN CURRY
with onion bhajis & chapatis

When you can't eat gluten, getting a takeaway curry can be a nightmare. You won't feel like you are missing out with this great alternative. If you're not gluten intolerant you can use ordinary flour for the bhajis. This version is quite mild but you can spice it up by adding more fresh chillies.

Serves 4, with 12-14 medium bhajis

Ingredients for the curry:
3 medium red onions, sliced
2.5 mm root ginger, sliced
1/2 bunch of fresh coriander, stalks only
(save the leaves for serving)
1 knob of butter
1 tbsp oil
1/2 fresh chilli, deseeded and finely sliced
2 tbsp curry paste (see page 156)
3-4 chicken thighs, meat cut off the bone
400g tin chopped tomatoes
400g tin chickpeas, drained
Few spoonfuls of natural yoghurt

Ingredients for the onion bhajis:
200g gluten-free flour
2 medium red onions, sliced
1/2 bunch of fresh coriander, roughly chopped
1 tsp cumin seeds
1 tsp salt
1 tsp chilli powder
1 tsp ground coriander
1/2 tsp bicarbonate of soda
1 tsp garam masala
1/2 chilli, finely sliced
125ml cold water
Vegetable oil, for shallow frying

To serve:
Natural yoghurt
Handful of coriander leaves, chopped
8 gluten-free chapatis (see page 26)

Gently fry the onion, ginger, coriander stalks and chilli in the butter and oil for about 10 minutes on a medium heat.

Add the curry paste and the chicken pieces, stirring well so that everything gets a good coating of the spices. Season with salt and pepper, and stir in the tinned tomatoes with half a tin of water.

Tip in the chickpeas and bring it to the boil then turn down the heat and let it simmer for 30 minutes or so. Stir regularly so that it doesn't stick, adding more water if necessary.

When the chicken is cooked through, have a taste and adjust the seasoning to your taste.

While the curry is cooking, make the chapatis and bhajis. For the bhajis, put all the dry ingredients in a bowl and mix them together with your hands until they're thoroughly combined, then pour in the water a bit at a time, as you don't want mixture to be too wet.

Heat about 4cm oil in a small deep pan on a medium to high setting. It should just start to show a few tiny bubbles at the bottom of the pan when it's hot enough.

Take a tablespoonful of the mixture and carefully place it in the oil. You can cook 2 at a time for about 2 minutes on each side, removing them when they're golden and placing them on a plate with a paper towel to soak up the excess oil.

Keep them warm in a low oven as you cook the rest. Do the same with the chapatis too.

Serve the curry with a dollop of natural yoghurt and the coriander scattered over, and the chapatis and bhajis on the side.

UNDER £4 FOR FOUR

CHICKEN PAELLA
with prawns & chorizo

There are so many versions of this traditional Spanish dish. In coastal areas, fish tends to be the dominant ingredient in paellas, whereas inland, they usually contain more meat, often rabbit as well as chicken. Every family has its own recipe, and as I'm one-sixteenth Spanish, I'm planning to pass this one down to mine.

Serves 4

Ingredients:
1 tbsp olive oil
1 onion, finely diced
1 carrot, finely diced
1 red pepper, deseeded and finely diced
1 tomato, finely diced
100g chorizo, sliced
2 garlic cloves , finely chopped
3-4 chicken thighs, meat cut off the bone
1 tsp paprika
750ml home-made chicken stock or using a
gluten-free stock cube
200g risotto or paella rice
1 tbsp tomato purée
100g frozen peas, defrosted
200g frozen prawns, defrosted

To serve:
Lemon wedges
Handful fresh flat-leaf parsley, chopped

Optional ingredients:
Pinch of saffron added to stock (optional)
You can add any other seafood you might
have; I often buy mixed bags of frozen to
keep in the freezer.

Heat the olive oil in a wide frying pan and cook the vegetables for 6-8 minutes or until they start to soften.

Add the chorizo and garlic and cook for a few more minutes, then add the chicken and the paprika.

In a saucepan, bring the stock to the boil and then remove it from the heat and add the saffron, if using, to infuse while you brown the chicken – this will take about 10 minutes.

Stir the rice into the chicken and vegetable pan and fry it for about 2 minutes, then add the tomato purée and half of the chicken stock.

Bring it to the boil then turn it down to a simmer. Stir it occasionally to stop it sticking to the bottom of the pan, but not too much as you don't want to break up the rice grains. Add a little more stock if necessary.

After 20 minutes the rice should be nearly cooked. At this point, pour in the rest of the stock along with the peas and prawns.

Place a lid on the pan and gently cook for 5 minutes more, by which time the rice should be al dente and all the stock absorbed.

Serve it with lemon wedges and parsley scattered over.

GLUTEN-FREE PIZZA
with a vegetarian topping

This recipe is suitable for vegetarians, but if you're a meat-eater, feel free to add chorizo, prawns or tuna if you have it in your store cupboard.

Serves 4 (makes 2 large pizzas)

Ingredients for the dough:
250ml milk
7g sachet dried yeast
2½ tsp caster sugar
400g gluten-free bread flour, plus extra for dusting
1 tsp xanthan gum
1 tsp salt
1 large egg
3 tbsp olive oil
½ tsp bicarbonate of soda
2 tsp cider vinegar

Ingredients for the tomato sauce:
1 garlic clove, finely sliced
1 tbsp olive oil
400g tin tomatoes
Squirt of tomato purée
Handful of fresh basil or 1 tsp dried

Ingredients for the topping:
Few handfuls of grated Cheddar
2 tomatoes, sliced
Mixed peppers, thinly sliced
1 red onion, thinly sliced
125g mozzarella, cut into chunks
A few olives

To make the pizza dough, heat the milk in a small pan until it's just lukewarm, then pour 50ml into a jug with the yeast and sugar. Mix it well and set it aside for a few minutes until it starts to bubble.

Meanwhile, sieve the flour and xanthan gum with the salt into a large bowl and make a well in the middle.

In a separate bowl, combine the egg, olive oil and the rest of the milk and pour this into the well, along with the yeast mixture. In a cup, whisk the bicarbonate of soda and vinegar together, and pour it into the well too. Gently mix everything together with a fork until it forms a dough.

Knead the dough briefly, then put it in an oiled bowl, cover it with a damp tea towel and leave it to prove in a warm place for around an hour, until it has doubled in size.

While it is proving, make the tomato sauce by briefly frying the garlic in oil and then tipping in the tinned tomatoes and purée, along with the basil and a good pinch of salt and pepper. Let it simmer gently for around 10 minutes, then blend it until it's smooth. Taste it and adjust the seasoning if necessary.

Preheat the oven to 220°C. Divide the dough into two pieces on a flour-dusted surface and roll them out to roughly 30cm in diameter and 3mm thick. Place them on lightly greased baking trays.

Spread the sauce thinly over the pizza base. Sprinkle over the cheese and sliced vegetables, followed by the mozzarella.

Bake the pizzas in the oven for 10-15 minutes or until the cheese is bubbling and the base is crisp.

PEA & MINT RISOTTO
with lemon zest

I used to be too scared to cook risotto. Everyone told me it was hard to make, so although I loved it and would often order it in restaurants, I had never made it myself until I started my blog. Well, now I know how easy it is, I have to stop myself adding it to every weekly meal plan.

Serves 4

Ingredients:
1 tbsp olive oil
Knob of butter
1 large onion, finely diced
1 carrot, finely diced
1 celery stalk, finely sliced
300g arborio risotto rice
1 litre stock, home-made or using a gluten-free stock cube, hot
150g frozen peas, defrosted
Handful of fresh mint, finely chopped
Zest and juice of 1 lemon
100g Cheddar or Parmesan, freshly grated

Optional ingredients:
50ml white wine

Fry the onions, carrot and celery in the oil and butter in a deep frying pan for around 15 minutes.

Add the rice and turn up the heat for a minute, stirring so as not to let it catch on the pan.

Pour in the wine, if you're using it, and after about a minute start adding the stock a ladleful at a time and stirring very gently on a medium heat.

You are waiting for each addition of stock to be absorbed before adding the next one.

After about 18-20 minutes, you should have used up the stock and the rice should be al dente. If it's still a bit hard, add a little more water.

When the rice is nearly ready add the peas, chopped mint, lemon zest and juice.

Just before serving, add the cheese and give it another stir to help it melt through the rice, then season to taste.

Keep back at least a third of the risotto (300g) as you will need it for another dish later in the week.

PATATAS BRAVAS
with salad

I recently read a book set in Spain and this seemed to be a dish the characters cooked regularly, so I found a version online and adapted it to fit within this week's food budget. Basically, it's just roast potatoes with a tomato and onion sauce, but who doesn't like midweek roasties? Thanks, Spain.

Serves 4

Ingredients for the patatas bravas:
900g potatoes, diced
3 tbsp olive oil
1 onion, finely chopped
3 garlic cloves, chopped
400g tin chopped tomatoes
1 tbsp tomato purée
2 tsp sweet paprika
1/4 tsp chilli powder
1/2 tsp sugar
Fresh parsley, to garnish

Ingredients for the salad:
2 large tomatoes, cut into chunks
1 small red onion, finely sliced
1/4 iceberg lettuce
1/4 cucumber, diced
1 carrot, finely sliced

Optional ingredients:
Sweet potatoes would also work well in this recipe

Preheat the oven to 200°C.

Put the potatoes in a roasting tin and toss them in 2 tbsp oil and some seasoning.

Roast them for about 40 minutes or until they are crisp and golden.

Meanwhile, make the sauce. Heat the remaining oil in a medium-sized saucepan and gently fry the onion for 5-7 minutes

Add the garlic, tomatoes, tomato purée, paprika, chilli powder, sugar and some salt and bring it to the boil, then reduce the heat and let it simmer, with the lid on, for 20 minutes – removing the lid for the last 10 minutes to allow the sauce to thicken, while stirring occasionally so it doesn't stick.

When the potatoes are ready, tip them into a dish and pour the hot sauce on top. Finish with a sprinkling of chopped parsley.

Serve them with the salad.

SPICY CHORIZO PASTA
with garlic bread

If you're gluten-free and like pasta you're limited to the few dried types available in supermarkets. I've never seen fresh gluten-free pasta. This recipe is for a simple home-made linguine type but if you're adventurous you can make any shape you like. See pages 16 and 19, or look online for some ideas.

Serves 4

Ingredients for the pasta:
300g gluten-free bread flour
2 tsp xanthan gum
2 eggs
1 tsp salt
1 tbsp oil
125ml water

Ingredients for the sauce:
3 tbsp olive oil
1 large onion, finely chopped
125g chorizo, sliced
3 garlic cloves, crushed
400g tin chopped tomatoes
1 tbsp tomato purée
1 tsp mixed herbs

To serve:
Home-made GF garlic bread (see page 155)

Optional ingredients:
Splash of red wine for the sauce
Handful of chopped fresh parsley to serve

To make the pasta, mix the flour and xanthan gum in a large bowl, then make a well in the middle. In a jug mix together the eggs, salt, oil and about a third of the water. Pour this mixture into the well and slowly bring the sides of the flour in on top of it and mix together well.

Gradually add the rest of the water until everything is combined, then knead the dough on a floured surface until it becomes springy. This should take about 10 minutes. Add a little more flour if the dough seems too wet.

Roll it out straight away with a rolling pin until it is very thin and almost translucent, and slice it into strips. Alternatively use a pasta machine if you have one. Leave your finished pasta on a lightly floured surface and cover it with a clean tea towel while you make the sauce.

Place a saucepan over a medium heat and soften the onions in the oil, then add the chorizo and cook for another 5 minutes.

Stir in the garlic, tomatoes, tomato purée, herbs, wine and a splash of water and simmer for around 10 minutes, until the sauce is thickened.

Meanwhile, bring a large pan of salted water to the boil and cook the pasta until it is al dente (6-8 minutes). Then drain it and return it to the pan and stir in the sauce. Sprinkle the chopped parsley on top and serve with some garlic bread.

ARANCINI
with salad & aioli

This traditional Italian dish is made with leftover risotto rice. You can imagine how it came about: from thrifty Italian housewives who were not prepared to throw away any perfectly good leftovers. Arancini can be eaten hot or cold. It is fun to make and looks impressive. The aioli works really well with it, but beware of the garlic – it'll keep the vampires away.

Serves 4

Ingredients for the arancini:
300g leftover risotto
100g Cheddar, diced
Large handful of gluten-free flour
1-2 eggs, whisked with a fork
3-4 gluten-free crusts, made into fresh
breadcrumbs
Oil, for deep-frying

Ingredients for the aioli:
2 egg yolks
2 garlic cloves
1 tsp lemon juice
70ml olive oil

Ingredients for the salad:
2 large tomatoes, cut into chunks
1 small red onion, finely sliced
1/4 iceburg lettuce
1/4 cucumber, diced
1 large carrot, finely sliced

Divide the risotto into golf ball-sized pieces. Put a cube of cheese in the centre of each ball and roll the rice around it. You should be able to make 12-14 of them.

In 3 shallow separate bowls, put the flour, the beaten egg and the breadcrumbs, seasoned with salt and pepper. Roll the rice balls firstly in the flour, then in the egg and finally in the breadcrumbs.

Heat the oil in a deep fat fryer or a large, deep saucepan to roughly 180°C. (To test the temperature if you don't have a thermometer, a cube of bread added to the oil should brown in about 40 seconds.)

Fry the rice balls in batches for 2-3 minutes, until they're crisp and golden. You can keep them warm in the oven while you cook the rest, and this will also help to melt the cheese even more.

To make the aioli, blend all the ingredients, except the olive oil, in a food processor, or with a hand blender. Continue to blend while pouring in a steady stream of oil, until it forms a thick sauce. Season to taste.

Serve with the salad.

LET US EAT CAKE

sweet treats

'Let them eat cake!' said Marie Antoinette when she heard that the French peasants had no bread to eat. The French queen is not remembered for her frugality but, if you know what you're doing, cake is a treat everyone can afford. By using leftovers and basic baking ingredients you won't break the bank. And I promise you these cakes will taste much better than anything you can buy from a supermarket.

PAVLOVA WITH FRUIT

Serves 8

Ingredients:
2 egg whites
100g sugar
Pinch of salt

To serve:
Fresh double cream
Seasonal fruit

Optional ingredients:
You can add any fruit you like,
or chopped, toasted nuts and melted
chocolate

Preheat the oven to 150°C.

Put the egg whites in a large, clean, dry bowl and beat them with a hand-held electric whisk until they form stiff peaks.

Gradually add the sugar and the salt, whisking continuously, until the mixture becomes thick and glossy.

Spoon or pipe the meringue onto greaseproof paper on a baking tray, then bake it for about 1 hour or until it's firm to the touch. Turn the oven off but leave the meringue inside to cool slowly for a chewier middle.

When it has cooled, whip some double cream and spoon it on top, along with some seasonal fresh fruit.

TREACLE TART

Makes 8 large slices

Ingredients for the pastry:
250g plain flour
Pinch of salt
130g butter, cubed (use margarine if vegan)
2-3 tbsp cold water

Ingredients for the filling:
400g golden syrup
150g-200g breadcrumbs
Zest and juice of 1 lemon

To make the short-crust pastry see page 44. Preheat the oven to 180°C and blind bake the base in a 20cm round cake tin.

While the pastry is cooking, make the filling by gently warming the syrup in a pan until it's runny, but not boiling.

Remove it from the heat and stir in the breadcrumbs and lemon zest and juice. Use more or less breadcrumbs to get the right consistency.

When the pastry is ready, pour in the treacle mixture and spread it on evenly. If you have any leftover pastry you can make a lattice top with strips of it. You'll need a little egg wash to help it brown.

Bake the tart in the oven for 25-30 minutes. Allow it to cool in the tin for a while before serving it.

LOUISE'S COCONUT SLICES
with raspberry jam

These coconut slices – rumoured to have been originally created for the wedding of Queen Victoria's daughter, Princess Louise, to the duke of Argyll – are popular in New Zealand, where are thought to have been introduced by British settlers. Desiccated coconut is a great stock cupboard ingredient that can be used for simple sweet treats, or in exotic curry recipes. As it's already dried it lasts for ages in an airtight container, ready for when you might need it again.

Makes 12-16 slices

Ingredients for the slices:
125g butter, softened
80g caster sugar
150g plain flour
1 tsp baking powder
2 egg yolks
200g raspberry or strawberry jam

Ingredients for the topping:
115g caster sugar
2 egg whites
85g desiccated coconut

Preheat the oven to 180°C.

Line a 18 x 28cm baking tin with baking paper. Make sure to leave paper hanging over the edges to help you remove the cake from the tin.

Beat the butter and sugar together, then stir in the flour and baking powder in a bowl until they are well combined.

Now add the egg yolks and stir until you have a soft dough.

Spoon the dough into the tin and smooth the surface with the back of the spoon.

Bake it for 12-15 minutes or until it has turned golden brown. Remove it from the oven and allow it to cool for 10 minutes before spreading the jam over it.

To make the topping, mix the sugar and desiccated coconut together in a bowl. Whisk the egg whites until they become glossier and form stiff peaks then fold them carefully into the sugar and coconut mixture.

Spread the topping over the jam layer and place the tin back in the oven to bake for about 25 minutes or until the top turns golden.

Allow the slice to cool in the tin before carefully taking it out and cutting it into pieces.

ANZAC BISCUITS

Anzac Day is a national day of remembrance in Australia and New Zealand that commemorates all Australians and New Zealanders who have served and died in wars and conflicts over the years. It has been claimed that these biscuits were sent by wives to soldiers abroad because they kept well during transportation.

Makes 24

Ingredients:
100g unsalted butter
100g caster sugar
1 tbsp golden syrup
1 tsp bicarbonate of soda
2 tbsp hot water
100g plain flour or gluten-free flour
85g desiccated coconut
85g porridge oats (not instant)

Optional ingredients:
20g pumpkin seeds
20g sunflower seeds
20g sesame seeds

Preheat the oven to 180°C and line 2 large baking sheets with baking parchment.

In a large saucepan, big enough to hold all of the ingredients, melt the butter, sugar and golden syrup together, then remove it from the heat.

In a bowl, dissolve the bicarbonate of soda in the hot water, then add it to the butter mixture in the saucepan. It will bubble up – don't be alarmed!

Now add the remaining ingredients to the saucepan and combine well.

Scoop tablespoonfuls of the mixture onto the lined baking sheets, leaving 2–3cm between each one to allow room for the biscuits to spread as they bake, then slightly flatten them with the back of the spoon.

Bake them until they're golden brown – 8–10 minutes – or longer if you want them crispy.

When cooked, the biscuits will still be slightly soft, but will harden to a chewiness once cooled.

EASY VANILLA BISCUITS

Makes at least 24

Ingredients:
100g butter, at room temperature
50g caster sugar
Few drops of vanilla extract
175g plain flour
2 tbsp milk

Optional ingredients:
Add chocolate chips or chopped dried fruit to the dough or decorate the cooked biscuits with icing and hundreds and thousands

Preheat the oven to 150°C.

Whisk together the butter and sugar in a bowl until they're light and fluffy. Stir in the vanilla, then add the flour and mix well. Next, add the milk and combine it with your hands to form a dough.

Chill it in the fridge for about 30 minutes if you have time.

Roll the dough out to about 5mm thick and cut it into circles. Alternatively, use a cutter of your choice as the biscuits hold their shape well during cooking. Prick the surface with the prongs of a fork.

Bake the biscuits on a greased baking sheet for 25 minutes or until they're golden brown. You can store them in an airtight box for up to a week.

HEALTHY BROWNIES

Makes 12

Ingredients:
250g pitted dates (cheaper to buy from the world food section of your supermarket)
125g mixed nuts
30g cocoa powder

Simply blend all the ingredients together in a food processor, then spread the mixture in a 20cm square tin, lined with baking parchments. Leave it in the fridge to set.

Chop it into squares to be enjoyed guilt-free.

To make the brownies a little less guilt-free you could drizzle over some melted chocolate.

ELDERFLOWER CAKE
using foraged flowers

I love the idea of foraging and getting wild food for nothing, even living in suburbia. Elder is a common shrub or tree that flowers in June. Make sure to pick the flowers on a sunny day for maximum sweetness. Of course, this light sponge is equally delicious made with shop-bought elderflower cordial – maybe just not quite as satisfying as making your own from scratch.

Makes 8 slices

Ingredients for the cake:
175g butter, softened, plus extra for greasing
175g caster sugar
3 eggs
140g self-raising flour
85g ground almonds
$\frac{1}{2}$ tsp baking powder
100ml milk

Ingredients for the drizzle:
4 tbsp elderflower cordial
(see below or buy from a supermaket)
4 tbsp white or golden granulated sugar

Elderflower cordial ingredients:
30 elderflower heads
3 pints boiling water
900g caster sugar
50ml juice from lemons
2 unwaxed oranges, sliced
3 unwaxed lemons, sliced

Preheat the oven to 160°C and grease and line a 20cm tin with greaseproof baking paper.

To make the cake mixture, whisk the butter and sugar until light and fluffy. Beat in the eggs, flour, almonds, baking powder and milk until smooth.

Tip the cake mixture into the tin and bake it for 45-50 minutes, using a skewer to test it's cooked through.

When the cake has come out of the oven, prick it all over with a cocktail stick.

Dissolve the sugar in the cordial and pour it over the cake while it's still warm.

Let it cool in the tin, then turn it out onto a wire rack.

To make the cordial, gently rinse the elderflowers to remove any dirt and bugs. Pour the boiling water over the sugar in a large mixing bowl, then add the lemon juice, the orange and lemon slices, and the flowers.

Leave it in a cool place for 24 hours, stirring occasionally.

Strain it through some muslin and transfer it to sterilised bottles.

FRUIT SCONES
with cream & jam

Jam first or cream first? Some say it depends whether you're eating them in Cornwall or Devon. I say it's up to you, either way is good. This version is simple to make – just don't make them too often or you'll be the size of Cornwall.

Makes 12

Ingredients:
250g self-raising flour
Pinch of salt
55g butter
25g caster sugar
125ml milk
80g dried fruit
1 orange for zest
1 beaten egg, to glaze (or use a little milk)

To serve:
Butter
Jam
Whipped or clotted cream

Heat the oven to 220°C and lightly grease a baking sheet.

Mix together the flour and salt, then rub in the butter. Stir in the sugar and then the milk to get a soft dough. Mix in the dried fruit. You can add more flour if the dough feels too wet.

Turn the dough onto a floured work surface and knead it very lightly. Roll it out to around 2cm thick.

Use a 5cm circular cutter to stamp out rounds and place them on the baking sheet.

Lightly knead together the rest of the dough and stamp out more scones to use it all up.

Brush the tops of the scones with the beaten egg. You could add a sprinkling of granulated sugar for a crunchy top.

Bake the scones for 12-15 minutes or until they're well risen and golden.

Cool them on a wire rack and serve them with cream or butter and jam.

ORANGE LOAF CAKE
with leftover vegetables

We all sometimes go to the supermarket and buy too many vegetables: either they come in a pre-packaged bag or you just over-estimate. In this recipe, you can use any root vegetable as long as the flavour isn't too strong – I wouldn't use celeriac. If you're using sweet vegetables like carrots or sweet potatoes you can cut back on the sugar. I'm including this cake in my 5-a-day...

Makes 12 large slices

Ingredients for the cake:
300g raw carrots, parsnips, pumpkin, squash or swede, peeled and grated
140g sultanas or raisins
Zest and juice of 1 orange
300g self-raising flour
250g light soft brown sugar
2 tsp mixed spice
1 tsp ground ginger
1 tsp bicarbonate of soda
4 large eggs, beaten
200g butter, melted, plus extra for greasing

Ingredients for the icing:
100g icing sugar, sifted
Zest and juice of 1 orange

Preheat the oven to 180°C and grease and line a 900g loaf tin with baking parchment.

In a bowl, mix the sultanas with the orange zest and microwave on high for 2 minutes.

In a separate bowl, combine the flour, caster sugar, spices, bicarbonate of soda and a pinch of salt with a fork.

Then add the eggs and melted butter to the sultana mixture. Beat it well and stir it into the bowl of dry ingredients.

Mix in the grated vegetables, and scrape it all into the tin with a spatula, making a dip in the middle so that it rises evenly.

Bake it for 40-50 minutes, or until a skewer inserted in the centre comes out clean. Let it cool in the tin.

Once it has cooled, sift the icing sugar into a bowl and stir in enough orange juice to make a runny icing. Drizzle it all over the cake and scatter the orange zest on top. Remove the cake from the tin once the icing has set.

MORAVIAN SUGAR CAKE
with leftover mashed potato

This traditional Moravian cake is a great way of using up leftover mashed potato – yes, you heard me right. The little sugar crystal pockets are a delicious surprise when you take a bite, and the spices make it taste luxurious and festive; but, like Christmas, it's not for every day. This is essentially a bread, which uses yeast and takes an hour to prove, so don't rush it. It will be worth the wait.

Makes 8 slices

Ingredients for the cake:
45g unsalted butter, plus extra for greasing
110g leftover mashed potato
190g plain flour, plus extra to dust
7g sachet fast-action dried yeast
$1/4$ tsp ground cinnamon
$1/4$ tsp freshly grated nutmeg
$1/4$ tsp fine salt
40g light brown soft sugar
Zest of $1/2$ orange
1 large egg
1 tsp vanilla extract

Ingredients for the topping:
$1/4$ tsp ground cinnamon
Zest of $1/2$ orange
5 tbsp light brown soft sugar
Pinch of fine salt
20g unsalted butter, melted

To serve:
Dusting of icing sugar

Options ingredients:
You can add a handful of any dried fruit, sultanas, chopped apricots, cranberries, etc

Lightly grease a 16cm round loose-bottomed cake tin with butter.

Whisk the mashed potato with 1 tbsp boiled water until it's smooth. In another bowl, mix together the dry ingredients with a fork.

In an electric mixer beat together the butter, sugar and orange zest for 2 minutes until creamy. Beat in the egg and the vanilla extract. Turning the mixer speed to low, add the flour mixture and the whisked potato a spoonful at a time.

When the dough is smooth and combined, scrape it out onto a floured work surface and knead it several times. It will still look a bit shaggy.

Place the dough in the prepared tin and press it into an even layer. Cover it with clingfilm and set it aside in a warm place for about 1 hour or until it has doubled in volume.

Meanwhile, preheat the oven to 180°C and make the topping by whisking all the ingredients together.

With a floury finger, poke 10-15 deep holes all over the surface of the cake dough 2-3cm apart, to the bottom of the tin. Fill each hole with a teaspoonful of the sugar mixture. Scatter the rest on top.

Bake the cake for 30 minutes or until it's puffed and golden and a skewer inserted in the centre comes out clean.

Let it cool in the tin before turning it out onto a wire rack.

VEGAN BERRY MUFFINS

Makes 8-10

Ingredients:
200g self-raising flour
150g sugar
$1/4$ tsp salt
2 tbsp baking powder
150ml soya milk
30ml vegetable oil
150g frozen berries, defrosted

Optional ingredients:
You can add dried fruit, cocoa powder
or vegan chocolate chips

Preheat the oven to 200°C and line a muffin tray with paper cases.

Combine the flour, sugar, salt and baking powder in a mixing bowl.

In a separate bowl blend the soya milk and oil. Then pour the mixture into the dry ingredients and beat them together.

Gently fold in the berries.

Spoon the mixture into the prepared tray and bake the muffins for 25-30 minutes, checking them after 20 minutes.

Allow them to cool on a wire rack.

FLAPJACKS

Makes 9-12

Ingredients:
125g butter
125g sugar
2-3 tbsp golden syrup
6-8 dried apricots, finely chopped
250g porridge oats

Preheat the oven to 180°C and grease a baking tray.

Melt the butter and sugar in a saucepan, then mix in the syrup, apricots and oats.

Give the mixture a good stir and pour it into the tray.

Press it down with the back of a spoon and bake it for 20 minutes or until it's golden brown.

Let it set before taking it out of the tray and cutting it into pieces.

BANANA BREAD
from leftover bananas

We sometimes have the odd banana or two that doesn't get eaten, so instead of throwing them away when the skin has gone brown, I make a batch of this banana bread to enjoy throughout the week. It keeps really well and is delicious with a cup of tea in the afternoon.

Makes one large loaf

Ingredients:
500g (3-5) ripe bananas
125g butter
125g brown sugar
2 eggs
200g plain flour
2 tsp baking powder
1 tsp bicarbonate of soda
1 tsp ground cinnamon
Pinch of salt
Oil
Handful of walnuts (optional)

Optional ingredients:
Pecans or hazlenuts instead of walnuts
1 tbsp maple syrup

Preheat the oven to 170°C and grease a 900g loaf tin.

If you are using walnuts, toast them in the oven for about 5 minutes and then roughly chop them.

Mash the bananas in a bowl and put them to one side while you make the rest of the mixture.

Cream the butter and sugar together with an electric whisk then beat in the eggs. Add the walnuts and bananas and mix well.

Sift in the flour, baking powder, bicarbonate of soda, cinnamon and salt and fold them into the mixture with a large metal spoon until you have a smooth batter.

Pour the mixture into the tin and bake it in the oven for about an hour, but check after 40 minutes with a skewer – if it comes out clean it is cooked.

Let the loaf cool for about 10 minutes, then remove it from the tin and transfer it to a wire rack. Store it in an airtight tin.

LUXURY CHRISTMAS DINNER
on a budget

When I first put my luxury 3-course £2.50 Christmas dinner on my blog, people said it couldn't be done and that I must have missed out half the ingredients. Well, I didn't. I even have smoked salmon to start and pigs in blankets to accompany the turkey. The prices may have gone up a bit since then, but if you stick to the recipes it will still come in very cheap.

Serves 8

Ingredients for the Christmas dinner:
1.2kg frozen turkey crown, defrosted
25 cocktail sausages
275g streaky bacon
1kg Brussels sprouts
1 tsp oil
50g cooked chestnuts, roughly chopped (optional)

Ingredients for the red cabbage:
1 red onions, sliced
1 apple, diced
Head of red cabbage sliced
1 tbsp sugar
Good splash red wine, (optional, can use water instead)
Good splash apple juice (optional)
2 tablespoons of balsamic vinegar
Salt and pepper

Ingredients for Christmas gravy:
Make as page 38 but instead of the Worcestershire sauce, onions and mustard add 2 tbsp cranberry sauce, not forgetting to double up the quantities

To serve:
Christmas stuffing (see page 40)
2kg potatoes for roasting (see page 37)
500g parsnips for roasting (see page 37)
500g carrots, cooked
Cranberry sauce

Firstly cook the turkey as per the packet instructions. As it's small you won't have to get up at some ridiculous hour to put it in the oven. There won't be much for leftovers, but who needs turkey curry, pie, stir-fry etc?

To make the pigs in blankets, wrap each cocktail sausage in half a rasher of streaky bacon. You can make the bacon go further by stretching it with the back of a knife. Cook them at about 200°C for 20-30 minutes or until the bacon is crispy. Save a bit of bacon for the Brussels sprouts.

Cook the sprouts in boiling water for 5 minutes, drain them, then roast them with 1 tsp oil, the chestnuts and some chopped bacon at 200°C for 30 minutes. (These can be done at the same time as the pigs in blankets).

For the red cabbage, melt the butter in a large saucepan and fry the sliced onion and apple for 10 minutes. Add the cabbage and all the other ingredients, then simmer for 30 minutes with the lid on. Season to taste. (You can make this the day before and heat it up in a microwave before serving.)

Place the carrots in a pan of cold water and bring it to the boil. Simmer for 5 minutes, then drain them and add a little butter and pepper before serving.

As you can see, we haven't skimped on any of the trimmings. You may not be able to stuff the turkey, but you can make some stuffing balls or a loaf instead. Bon appetit!

SMOKED SALMON MOUSSE

Serves 8

Ingredients:
200g cream cheese
240g smoked salmon trimmings
1 lemon
Pinch of salt and pepper
80g watercress
Brown bread

Using a blender, blitz $^3/_4$ of the salmon with the cream cheese and 1 tsp lemon juice, and season to taste.

With this mixture, you'll make 8 individual mousses. For each, place a piece of clingfilm on a clean surface and drop a dessert spoonful of it in the middle. Wrap the clingfilm round it and roll it into a ball. Squash the balls into eggcups or an old egg box.

Put the mousses in the fridge for a few hours to firm up.

When you are ready to eat, transfer them to plates. You can decorate them with the reserved slivers of salmon and the watercress.

I like to garnish them with a twisted slice of lemon, and serve them with a few triangles of bread and butter.

CHRISTMAS PUDDING

Ingredients:
200g butter
2 tbsp black treacle
100g breadcrumbs
100g self-raising flour
2 tbsp baking powder
200g dried apricots and prunes, chopped
300g mixture of currants, sultanas and raisins
100g soft brown or muscavado sugar
1 cooking apple, finely grated
1 medium carrot, finely grated
3 tsp mixed spice
1 tsp ground ginger
1 tsp ground cinnamon
$\frac{1}{2}$ tsp nutmeg
$\frac{1}{2}$ tsp salt
Juice and rest of 1 lemon or orange
3 tbsp brandy (optional)

Cream the butter and treacle together with an electric whisk.

Add all the other ingredients and mix. You should have a soft dropping consistency.

Pour the mixture into a greased microwavable basin, leaving a gap of 2-3cm at the top to allow it to rise.

Cover the basin with a circle of greaseproof paper and place a saucer on top.

Microwave the pudding on a high setting for about 15 minutes, checking after 10. It could require longer, depending on the size of the basin. Stick a skewer in the centre to see if it comes out clean.

Serve the pudding warm with cream or custard.

Index:

Acknowledgements:

I'd like to thank my husband Phil who calmly took all my food photos, originally for my blog and later for this book. Also Avril for inspiring me to start my blog in the first place, and correcting my appalling grammar. To Emily and Ruth for being my willing guinea pigs. To everyone who visited my blog, and has supported me and encouraged me to do more, especially Pesala. Lastly, Rebecca and Aurea and the team at Short Books.

Jane Ashley is a graphic designer who lives with her husband and daughter in London. She was inspired to try feeding her family on an extraordinarily tight budget after volunteering at a night shelter and having to produce nutritious, low-cost meals. Find her blog at eatnotspend.wordpress.com